Rich? Stockton
1730–1781

Portrait by George Washington Conarroe,
after a painting by John Wollaston c. 1876.
Courtesy Independence National Historical Park Collection.
(Also cover image)

RICHARD STOCKTON

HIS SACRED HONOR
JUDGE RICHARD STOCKTON
A Signer of The Declaration of Independence

JOHN C. GLYNN, JR.
&
KATHRYN GLYNN

RICHARD STOCKTON
National Statuary Hall Collection,
United States Capitol

Published by Hereditea
Brentwood, Tennessee
Book Design by Melissa Solomon
Nashville, Tennessee
ISBN: 978-0-9796029-0-0 (Formerly: ISBN-13: 978-0-9777623-1-6/ISBN-10: 0-9777623-1-9)

Dedication

IN MEMORY OF BARBARA JEAN GLYNN
WHO STARTED US ON THIS JOURNEY

Table of Contents

Forward

Judge Richard Stockton personified the principles of sacrifice in defense of his beliefs as well as any American that has ever lived. He paid the supreme price for placing his signature on the Declaration of Independence and pledging his life, his fortune and his Sacred Honor. The signing of this immortal document placed those men in one of the darkest and most perilous periods of history in this country, and I hope to illuminate the sacrifices some of the signers endured. As a direct descendant of Judge Richard Stockton I thought I knew about him until I started this book. I soon realized I had much to learn about his life and the hardships he endured.

The purpose of this book is to tell the story of Judge Richard Stockton, my fifth great grandfather. Judge Richard Stockton was the only signer to be imprisoned as a common criminal, put in irons, and subjected to brutal treatment at the hands of the British while a prisoner in New York the winter of 1776-1777. I have tried to be historically accurate, and my hope is that you will gain knowledge of how Richard Stockton and other patriots during this period of the Revolutionary War suffered for the freedom many take for granted today.

I am a member of an organization called the Descendants of the Signers of the Declaration of Independence (DSDI). We meet at different locations three times a year but always in Philadelphia on the 4th of July in Independence Hall. There we hold a meeting, read the Declaration of Independence out loud, and descendants rise as their

KATHRYN AND JOHN GLYNN
LECTURE AT HISTORIC MORVEN
"Richard Stockton's Honor"
Princeton, grand opening of the Museum, 2004.

signer's name is called. At the Philadelphia meeting in 2004 I was asked to give a speech at our annual black tie dinner on my signer, Judge Richard Stockton. After the speech the president of the DSDI took me aside and asked me if I had read a new book about the Revolutionary War and told me I would not like what the author said about my ancestor.

July 4th 2005 I addressed the DSDI at our meeting in Independence Hall a place that I felt appropriate. My speech follows:

I would like to thank President General Thomas Hayward for allowing me to speak today. I am here to say a few words on a subject that I am very passionate about...Honor! I have served this country under arms for 42 years and I am still serving. I am here to defend my 5th great-grandfather's sacred honor as he is being accused of being a turncoat and infamous by a well-known author of American history.

Judge Richard Stockton, like your ancestor, was an honorable patriot who pledged his life, fortune and Sacred honor to the cause of freedom. He never gave up on independence or supported the crown and was certainly never a turncoat.

Last year after I spoke on the life of my ancestor Richard Stockton, I was asked by our past president Sandy Stromberg if I had read *Washington's Crossing* as I would not like what the author, David Hackett Fischer, wrote about my ancestor and he was right. I have done extensive research on Richard Stockton's life including his capture in November 1776 and release from prison in January 1777. I corresponded with Mr. Fischer, and according to him, his source for calling him infamous and a turncoat was a March 17, 1777 letter from John Witherspoon to his son David. He quoted a small part of the letter talking about Stockton and said he "believed" from this that Stockton took the oath of allegiance to the King. This is not true; this is not what Witherspoon wrote in his letter, he wrote only about rumors being spread about Judge Stockton as is evident if you read the entire letter. I pointed this out and other errors in his book including his cited references and our correspondence stopped. I do not blame John Witherspoon as he was only writing a personal letter to his son on events in Princeton and rumors being spread about Judge Stockton and never imagined that 229 years later this letter about rumors would be used to attack the character of his good friend Richard Stockton.

I have written a rebuttal that I believe shows that Richard Stockton was the great patriot we all know. I think you will agree that misinformation can hurt us all. My concern is that these untruths are being spread in some current books, and the reading public will accept them as the truth. As an example, on our tour today, our guide told me "Isn't it interesting that after signing the Declaration of Independence Richard Stockton had taken Howe's protection." I told him it was not true and asked him where his information came from; he replied "Washington's Crossing."

Starting today I am defending Richard Stockton's sacred honor and character, here in this place of honor to us, descendants of these brave signers of our Declaration of Independence. We must defend their sacred honor against attacks as they are not here to defend themselves.

Thank You.

I received a rousing round of applause and after the meeting many told me "Good for you" and "We are with you".

You might say the Declaration of Independence and the American Revolution are in my blood as I am also related to other signers Thomas Nelson Jr., John Adams, Samuel Adams, Thomas Jefferson (cousins), and Benjamin Rush (uncle by marriage). I share the same great grandfather, Captain Nicolas Martiau of Yorktown Virginia, with General George Washington (cousin) and Queen Elizabeth II of England (twice a cousin), and I directly descend from King Robert Bruce of Scotland who, like George Washington, fought to win independence from the British. I also descend from four signers of the Declaration of Arbroath, the Scottish

Declaration of Independence of 1320 - "For, as long as but a hundred of us remain alive, never will we on any condition be brought under English rule. It is in truth not for glory, nor riches, nor honours that we are fighting, but for freedom–for that alone, which no honest man gives up but with life itself."

My wife Kathryn and I dress in period 1776 clothing and speak to organizations and schools about the Declaration of Independence and Richard and Annis Boudinot Stockton. We want to renew interest in the Declaration of Independence for without this document, the sacrifices of the 56 men who signed it, and the brave patriots who fought the Revolutionary War, we would not have a constitution or a free country today. My hope is that after reading this book you will want to learn more about all the signers of the Declaration of Independence and the Revolutionary War. As Abigail Adams wrote to her husband John, "Posterity, who are to reap the blessings, will scarcely be able to conceive the hardships and sufferings of their ancestors." The more we learn of our history and understand how we got to where we are, the better off we will be as a country.

I would like to say that without the support, research, typing and personal effort of Kathryn, my lovely wife of 40 years, this book would not be possible.

John C. Glynn, Jr.
Nashville, Tennessee

INTRODUCTION

Judge Richard Stockton, like most men of his era, lived and died by his word and his honor. In *The Signers of the Declaration of Independence* published in 1930 by Prudential Press, it is written of Judge Richard Stockton: "History may give more space to other of the Revolutionary heroes, but none deserves greater honor. Conscientious, upright, just and wise, Richard Stockton survives. His fair fame and his active and varied life have been a conspicuous mark for those who seek evidence of honored patriotism and sterling Americanism. His name will always attract the love and affection of his countrymen, and his example will ever wield over them a powerful influence."

The following was taken from *American Prisoners of War* by Danske Dandridge Dec. 6, 1910:

It is for the sake of the martyrs of the prisons themselves that this work has been executed. It is because we, as a people, ought to know what was endured; what wretchedness, what relentless torture, even unto death, was nobly borne by the men who perished by thousands in British prisons and prison ships of the Revolution; it is because we are in danger of forgetting the sacrifice they made of their fresh young lives in the service of their country; because the story has never been adequately told, that we, however unfit we may feel ourselves for the task, have made an effort to give the people of America some account of the manner in which these young heroes, the flower of the land, in the prime of their vigorous manhood, met their terrible fate.

Too long have they lain in the ditches where they were thrown, a cart-full at a time, like dead dogs, by their heartless murderers, unknown, unwept, unhonored, and unremembered. Who can tell us their names? What monument has been raised to their memories?

It is true that a beautiful shaft has lately been erected to the martyrs of the Jersey prison ship. But it is improbable that even the place of interment of the hundreds of prisoners who perished in the churches, sugar houses, and other places used as prisons in New York in the early years of the Revolution, can now be discovered. We know that they were, for the most part, dumped into ditches dug on the outskirts of the little city, the New York of 1776. Little did these young men think that they were, in some cases, literally digging a grave for themselves.

More than a hundred and thirty years have passed since the victims of Cunningham's cruelty and rapacity were starved to death in churches consecrated to the praise of worship of a God of love. It is a tardy recognition that we are giving them, and one that is most imperfect, yet it is all that we can do. The ditches where they were interred have long been filled up, built over, and intersected by streets. Who of the multitude that daily pass to and fro over the ground that should be sacred ever give a thought to the remains of the brave men beneath their feet, who perished that they might enjoy the blessings of liberty?

Republics are ungrateful; they have short memories; but it is due to the martyrs of the Revolution that some attempt should be made to tell to the generations that succeed them who they were, what they did, and why they suffered so terribly and died so grimly, without weakening, and without betraying the cause of that country which was dearer to them than their lives.

It is a solemn and affecting duty that we owe to the dead, and it is in no light spirit that we, for our part, begin our portion of the task. (Dandridge IX)

This is as true today as the day Danske Dandridge wrote this nearly one hundred years ago. This is why we endeavored to write our book about Judge Richard Stockton and other patriots of the American Revolution, to honor their sacrifices.

The Beginning
Date: July 1, 1776

Hammering hooves fell ever forward upon the muddy, washed-out road. Muscles flexed, sinews stretched with rhythmic consistency. The horsemen, crouched, blurred silhouettes upon the road, spurred their steeds onward, with whip and call, through the failing light. Bone white fingers of lightning crawled across the sky as the daylight retreated to rolling blackness. Rain stung and wind howled as they pressed steadily on.

The horsemen were close friends, Judge Richard Stockton and Rev. John Witherspoon. They traveled from Princeton to Philadelphia to hear the case for the Declaration of Independence as New Jersey's newly elected members of Congress.

Upon arrival, the Judge and the Reverend threw open the State House doors, their black boots muddied to the knees. Their clothing was soaked through. The storm had delayed them, and the meeting was well under way. John Adams, a prominent supporter for declaring independence, was concluding his speech. The two New Jersey delegates made their way to their seats and the commotion subsided. Then, Richard stood and beseeched Adams to repeat what they had missed. Adams refused; he had been interrupted and was, no doubt, vexed by the appeal. Richard requested a second time and with the admonition of several colleagues, Adams acquiesced.

John Adams rose and delivered an impassioned oration that kindled embers in the hearts of many men present. There was then a great debate over the matter. In the end, Richard stood and proclaimed his full support for the Declaration of Independence with a grim notion of what lay ahead for himself, his family, his fellow congressmen, and what would become his country. The fate of the colonies would be forever altered. The struggle for freedom had begun.

THE JOURNEY NORTH

It was a cold, crisp morning the 29th of November 1776. A chilling wind was blowing the last remaining leaves from the trees and swirling them across the road. The magnificent black stallion was galloping at full speed for Princeton, New Jersey with his master gently urging him on. The rider was Richard Stockton, a lawyer, and former Judge of the Supreme Court of New Jersey, now a member of the Continental Congress and a signer of the Declaration of Independence. He was six feet tall, of slender build, with gray green eyes and handsome in appearance. He was an accomplished horseman, a skilled swordsman, and he was riding to save his family from the British army. He knew, as a signer of the Declaration of Independence, that he and his young family would be in grave danger if they fell into British hands.

Stockton had been north to Ticonderoga, Saratoga and Albany, New York on a mission from Congress and had spent nearly two months with General Philip Schuyler and the Continental Army. From Ticonderoga on November 10th, 1776 Richard wrote to John Hancock, the President of the Congress, that he and fellow signer George Clymer had "gone through with their business." He finished his report and sent it to Congress. He immediately set out for Princeton and traveled South down the Hudson Valley.

The deeply rutted roads were muddy and difficult for his horse, but he pressed on with great urgency. On November 23rd, Richard was appointed by Congress to another congressional committee of five to see that the Board of War attended to the pressing business of sending reinforcements to Washington. It would seem that John Hancock and Congress were pleased with the work of Richard Stockton, since they continued to assign him difficult responsibilities.

The journey had been long and it was physically and mentally exhausting for him. He was deeply concerned about the safety of his family with every battle report that reached him. He learned in October of the defeat at White Plains then of the capture of Fort Washington on November 16, and now of the recent evacuation of Fort Lee. As Richard hurried south, Washington was retreating from New York to Newark, New Jersey.

> On the road as he approached Princeton, he happened upon some of the ragged, hungry, demoralized soldiers of Washington's defeated army on their retreat from New York. Richard rode up to the officer in charge and introduced himself as a member of Congress; he told the officer that he was on his way to Princeton to move his family from danger. (Sanderson 3: 100)

The officer was General Nathaniel Heard from nearby Monmouth County and he remembered Richard Stockton from his days as a well respected judge. He told Richard that his mission was to secure boats for the army to cross the Delaware River in the event the continental army had to retreat to Philadelphia. General Heard said the British army would be close behind and recommended that Richard quickly gather his family and leave Princeton or risk capture by the British. Richard told him he was taking his family to a friend's home thirty miles east in Freehold located in Monmouth County. General Heard informed Richard that General Washington had recently assigned a battalion of his men to that area due to a loyalist uprising. The uprising had been suppressed, and he considered it as good a choice as any for locating the family, as loyalists were everywhere and the battalion's presence would hopefully diminish loyalist activities in the area. He suggested Stockton

THE STOCKTON MANSION.

Morven

HOME OF JUDGE RICHARD STOCKTON AND HIS WIFE ANNIS BOUDINOT STOCKTON
Courtesy Morven Museum and Garden

not go south, as that was the direction General Washington would take to protect Philadelphia. The British would follow Washington and his army, and people were already deserting that city.

The fact that General Washington and his army were close by in Newark, only thirty miles north of Princeton and Freehold, and the battalion stationed in Monmouth County helped solidify his decision to take his family to Freehold. Richard bid General Heard Godspeed and galloped the few miles to Princeton.

As Richard arrived in Princeton his heart was lightened as he saw his beloved home "Morven", and Samuel his trusted servant hurried to greet him and take his horse. As he opened the door and called out, his lovely wife Annis hurried down the stairs to embrace him, and the children rushed to greet their loving father who had been absent from them nearly two months. Annis was overjoyed to see her dear husband at last and know he was safely away from the British army; she worried that the British might have taken him captive while he traveled in New York with the Continental army. Richard was thankful that they were all safe but knew they must be quick to leave. He told them it was best they leave Princeton and go stay with their good friend, John Covenhoven. The family had stayed with Covenhoven before, and they quickly gathered what they would need for the trip. The twins, Mary and Susan, at fifteen were old enough to know they were in danger, but eight-year-old Lucius and three-year-old Abigail thought a trip would be great fun.

Richard learned from Annis, that Governor Livingston and the legislature had already fled to Trenton, then on to Burlington. The town was quickly becoming a ghost town. Annis had been packing as she anticipated their removal from Movern, but she didn't want to alarm the children until she heard from Richard and she was certain he would come for them.

Their oldest son John Richard, a lad of 13, but already a young man of sensibility convinced Richard and Annis that he should be left in charge of Movern along with their trusted servant Samuel. John Richard argued they must not leave their home vacant for looters to destroy, and if he stayed with Samuel, he would say that his family was away on business, and he was in charge of the house in their absence. Reluctantly they agreed and waited until the last possible moment to leave their beloved home and brave young son.

Before Richard arrived in Princeton, Annis had learned of the British army's advance and secretly had gone to Nassau Hall (College of New Jersey), gathered the papers of the Whig Society and other important political documents that had been placed in Nassau Hall for safe-keeping during the Revolutionary War. The documents were known to Annis as she was well informed on all the political questions of the day and was also acquainted with her husband's political correspondence. A few years before, he had written: "I have left my letters to the Governor open that you may see their contents. As soon as you peruse them, enclose the gazettes, seal the packet, and send them on immediately." (Stockton, J.W. 9) Knowing the disastrous results that would ensue from these important papers falling into the hands of the British, she buried them with her own hands under a tree near the house. It was an act that was not forgotten by the all-male Whig Society, as she was later made the only woman member of the American Whig Society. (9)

Annis was a poet who wrote about the cultural and political tensions of her time. She was admired by her friends for her writing ability, and some of her poems had been published as early as 1758. She left her own treasured papers in their library, which was regarded as one of the finest in the colonies and hoped they would be overlooked by the British if they did come to Morven as she had no time to gather them.

Richard remained at Movern rendering aid to the Continental army as they passed by, until he could no longer expose his family to the approaching danger of the British army, and they had a long journey ahead of them. Princeton was practically deserted now as Richard instructed John Richard and Samuel to give the remaining food to the rest of the Continental army if they came through town and keep and hide only what they would need for their future use, as he knew the British Army would take everything left behind.

They quickly loaded the coach with the clothes they would need and tied his prized black stallion to the back. They all gathered around and hugged John Richard, then climbed into the coach. Annis and the girls tearfully waved goodbye, and Richard sat in the front seat to drive the horses. Richard and Annis prayed they had made the right decision to leave him behind. Other than being the home of the College of New Jersey, Princeton was a small town with little to offer the British, and Richard hoped they would quickly pass through on their march to Philadelphia.

As they settled in the coach for the long journey, Mary and Susan tried to make light of the trip, and they sang and helped care for the younger children. They stopped midway and had a quick meal Annis had packed for them, rested the horses, and were on their way again. The wind was chilling as the day wore on, and they wrapped themselves in warm blankets as the sun dipped below the horizon and evening fell. The moonlight guided them along the winding road and at last they saw their destination with the candles burning brightly in the windows. It was a long and exhausting journey, and Richard was thankful when they finally reached "Federal Hall" the home of John Covenhoven late the night of November 29, 1776.

THE CAPTURE

In September, before Richard started on his journey north, he and John Covenhoven made an agreement that should the British army at anytime head toward Princeton, Richard's family should go stay with John, and should the British head to Freehold, John and his family would go to Princeton. The path of the British was now set upon Princeton, and John graciously welcomed them to his home. His wife Eleanor and his children were glad to see them. Richard saw to it that his horses were cared for as he took great pride in them and then he carried their satchels containing their clothes and belongings into the two adjoining rooms their host had provided for them. They had been friends for a number of years and John and his family were frequent guests of the Stockton's at Movern. John had food and drink ready for them, even though it was well past dinner time. They enjoyed a hearty meal of hot soup, bread, cheese, sliced ham and apple pie. It had been a long day and Susan and Mary helped the younger children prepare for bed. Annis and Eleanor visited and expressed their concerns about the war, but before long Annis, weary from the journey, retired for the night.

Richard and John talked on into the night as they were both concerned about the state of the army. Richard had seen this Continental army first hand and knew they were in dire need of everything. He also knew they had fought bravely and he was proud of their courage. In August before Richard left for New York with George Clymer, George Washington had an army of 20,000. In the past three months Washington had lost four battles - at Brooklyn, Kips Bay, White Plains, and Fort Washington and had just given up Fort Lee without a fight. Washington now had only about 3,500 men under his command. His men were broken and dispirited. They had no tents, and every pick and shovel had been left behind at Fort Lee. Many were without shoes, and few had warm coats. The Continental army had lost as prisoners 329 officers and 4101 enlisted men, during the past twelve weeks. Richard and John hoped that General Washington would turn the tide of war, as they both had great respect for him. Richard knew Washington personally and thought he was the one man that could lead this young country to victory.

John Covenhoven served as Vice President of the New Jersey state legislature and told Richard that Adjutant-General Joseph Reed, Richard's close friend and former law student, now Washington's closest advisor had dispatched to Governor William Livingston on November 24th with the urgent request that he and the legislature of New Jersey, should urge forward with new recruits for the army. As a result of Adjutant-General Reed's efforts, an act was passed by the Council and General Assembly of New Jersey to organize four battalions of state troops by embodying volunteers from the militia of the different counties. However, they could not raise any volunteers, as no one wanted to face the dreaded British army.

Richard and John both agreed that the people of New Jersey as well as the other states would have to rise to the needs of their army, and without the help of the people, liberty would surely be lost. They spoke of what a fine man General Joseph Reed was, and what a brave and model officer he was, as well as an accomplished gentleman. No man was more freely admitted to the confidence and counsel of General Washington than Reed, and to no man did Washington more frequently refer for advice. When a British diplomat, tried to bribe Reed to return to the support of the English crown, Reed replied "I am not worth purchasing, but such as I am, the King of Great Britain is not rich enough to do it."(Stryker 7)

The next day many of John's friends, hearing of Washington's retreat from Newark, stopped by to advise him of the developments. Richard and John would have preferred that Richard's whereabouts be kept secret, but word traveled quickly, and soon everyone knew that the Honorable Richard Stockton and family were guests of the Covenhoven's.

Colonel David Forman and his battalion from General Nathaniel Heard's brigade were quartered nearby as they had been sent by Washington to "apprehend all persons who appear to be concerned in any plot or design against the liberty or safety of the United States."(Stryker 9) It was reported that two-thirds of New Jersey were Loyalists, and "Black David," as he was called, full of energy and merciless severity was the very man to suppress a loyalist conflict around his own county. He captured and questioned many men, doing his work quickly and with great effect. Richard and John felt reasonably safe with Forman and his troops near by, but they still discussed the possibility of escape by sea if the British army turned in their direction. Covenhoven had close connections with ship owners up and down the coast and had made arrangements for their escape if necessary, but for the time being they decided to wait and see which direction the British army would move, believing it would be south to Philadelphia. The day quickly passed to evening as the families visited, took meals together and tried to decide what should be their next course of action.

The night of November 30th turned bitterly cold. The wind howled as Richard bid John a goodnight and finally settled into bed. Winter weather was taking hold of New Jersey, and he was thankful he had found a warm and safe place for his family to stay. His oldest daughter Julia, had married Dr. Benjamin Rush, also a signer of the Declaration of Independence, in January and was expecting their first child. Richard prayed they were out of harm's way, as they lived in Philadelphia, and he fully believed the British Army would try to capture Philadelphia and the members of Congress along with it. He was sure Benjamin would take Julia and find safety with his family outside of Philadelphia. He worried about young John Richard and Samuel back at Morven and hoped they had made the right decision to leave the brave lad behind. Once in the warm bed he held Annis close and tried to comfort her, as she was worried about their family. As he struggled to put their minds at ease, his weary body and mind finally found the sleep he so desperately needed.

Suddenly in the darkness came voices, then shouting, and as Richard realized something was dreadfully wrong, the door burst open and in rushed a mob of angry men with guns and swords drawn. He sprung from the bed but before he could react, they were upon him, beating him with their fists and gun butts and knocking him to the floor where they continued to attack him. Annis ran around the bed and threw herself over Richard to stop the beating, but they roughly shoved her out of the way, and she slid across the floor and into a wall, but she quickly picked herself up. The loud voices woke the children sleeping in the next room, and they ran in to see what was causing the disturbance. Annis ran over and gathered the children to her and tried to quiet them as they cried and pleaded with the men to do their father no further harm. Richard's first concern was for Annis and the children, and he reasoned with the men to take him and leave the family in peace. After much discussion and additional blows from the angry mob of Loyalists, amid cries of "traitor", they decided to do as he asked, as they had their prize, a member of Congress and a signer of the Declaration of Independence, and had no need of women and crying children.

The sight of his young children crying and clinging to each other in fear was heartbreaking. Annis and the children were then ordered into the next room. Annis refused to leave Richard as she feared for his life, and she told Mary and Susan to care for young Abigail and Lucius and take them into the next room. Young Lucius, only eight years old, wiped tears from his eyes and summoning all the courage he could, sternly told the men they had better not hit his father anymore, which brought a glare from the nearest Loyalist. Susan quickly put her arm around him and pulled him from the room.

Annis stood her ground and refused to leave Richard. She was told their quarrel was not with her, but with the traitor. Richard begged her to please go with the children as they would need her, and there was no need for them both to be taken prisoner. After a few anxious moments their eyes met and reluctantly, without shedding a tear the brave Annis did as he asked, but as she passed him she leaned down and brushed the blood from his cheek with her hand and their eyes spoke what their lips could not. She quietly left the room and closed the door behind her never losing her composure.

Richard was not allowed to dress properly for the cold weather, and was only allowed to pull on his breeches and stockings that were draped over a chair. As he reached for his fine boots next to the chair, they were snatched from him by one of the men who removed his old worn out shoes, and threw them at Richard to put on. The loyalist mob quickly gathered up all his belongings and clothes in the satchels stacked around the bedroom, and took them for their own use. His hands were bound with a rope, and he was struck with fists and rifle butts as he and John Covenhoven were pushed into the cold night. His fellow countrymen, now his captors, were delivering him to the British in Perth Amboy. His loyalist captors had taken them in the dead of night and planned to march them on a little traveled road for fear of being seen by any of Forman's troops camped nearby.

His captors now rode his magnificent black stallion and took his other fine horses to pull a wagon piled full of Richard and John's stolen belongings. He and John were made to walk tied behind the wagon clad only in their nightshirts and breeches on the muddy and now freezing road. As the night wore on, it started to rain then turned into a freezing sleet that soaked their thin garments. Their captors rode on horseback with hats and warm cloaks shielding them from the freezing weather.

Several times he and John slipped and fell only to be pulled through the mud until they could pull themselves to their feet. Somewhere along the road, he lost the old shoes in the mud and had to continue on without them. He and John were cold, hungry and exhausted from their ordeal, but when the men at last stopped for a rest after several hours they did not offer their prisoners any of their food or drink. Richard and John collapsed next to a stout tree and tried to get shelter from the howling wind.

Richard thought about John who was a bit overweight and gasping to catch his breath. When one of the men approached, Richard asked if they might have something to eat or drink. The man walked over as if he was going to share his cup with them then laughed as he gave Richard a swift kick to the ribs. No food or drink for the traitors was his order. Richard had never in his life been treated with such brutality, nor had he ever been so cold, exhausted or hungry. He did not recognize any of them, but he was well known to many men of New Jersey as he had been a Royal Supreme Court judge for many years before he renounced his allegiance to King George, took his place in the Continental Congress, and signed the Declaration of Independence.

With two thirds of the population of New Jersey loyal to the King, the Loyalists felt Richard Stockton, as a signer of the Declaration of Independence, would be convicted of high treason against the King. The penalty for high treason was the barbarous punishment of hanging, drawing, and quartering. This punishment would be a strong deterrent to the Rebel army of Washington. One of John Covenhoven's neighbors had informed the loyalist mob of his location. That man would eventually be punished for this crime against one of America's founding fathers.

After the agonizing march through the night and into the next day, they were delivered to the British at the jail in Perth Amboy. The British jailer in charge was told that Richard Stockton was a traitor to the King, a member of Congress, and a signer of the Declaration of Independence. Richard and John were immediately clapped in heavy irons on their wrists and ankles to prevent their escape and thrown into a cold dark cell with several other prisoners. They would be shown no mercy and would now be treated as common criminals.

The cold floor was covered with soiled straw that smelled of urine and human waste. Richard and John had been without food for nearly two days, and when he again asked for something to eat, he was told they could starve for all their British captors cared. They were finally allowed to drink some putrid water from a bucket. Richard was bloody from the gashes on his face and arms, wounds he had received as he tried to shield himself from the rifle butts that had been used to beat him, and his feet were in terrible shape from the march. Thankfully, John had not been beaten as severely, although he was in poor shape. They pulled their mud stained nightshirts to cover them from the cold and tried to keep warm on the hard floor in the freezing cell. The cell was so crowded that there was not room to lie down, the men had to sleep sitting up holding their knees to their chest.

Richard and John were men of high social standing and means and had never been subject to such uncivilized treatment. After several days of brutal treatment with no food, no blankets or warm clothing to keep the cold away, Richard was taken to the notorious Provost Prison in New York. It was decided by the British officers in Perth Amboy, that as a member of Congress and a signer of the Declaration of Independence, Richard should be sent to New York. They felt the British officers there would be the better judges of what fate should hold for him. When Richard was led into the Provost prison, the whole guard was paraded and he was delivered over to Cunningham and questioned by him.

The Perth Amboy jail was horrible, but conditions in the Provost Prison were even worse. His plight was now fighting cold and starvation. In one of the coldest winters recorded, "there was not a pane of glass in the windows, and nothing to keep out the cold except the iron grates." (Sanderson 156) The prisoners had rags for clothes and no blankets. Most of the prisoners were walking skeletons…overrun with lice from head to foot. A fire might be built every three days to cook their meager piece of pork or heat the disgusting watery soup. One of the prisoners told Richard that out of sixty-nine men taken with him, only fifteen were still alive, and eight of those were sick.

The British army's Provost Marshal William Cunningham, a brutish man and hater of patriots was in charge of the New York Prisons. He starved more than 2000 prisoners outright when he sold their rations and even laced the remaining flour with arsenic. He was known to drag

INTERIOR OF THE OLD JERSEY PRISON SHIP IN THE REVOLUTIONARY WAR
Engraving by Edward Bookhout, 1855
Library of Congress Prints and Photographs Division Washington DC: cph 3a09150

select war prisoners to the gallows bound and gagged, and hang them without charges or trials. Over 250 were executed in this manner, and thousands more died from starvation and his abuse in the prisons. Over 11,000 prisoners would die on the prison ships, and thousands more died in the prisons in New York compared to 4,435 soldiers that died in combat over the entire six years of war. (Sanderson 158)

Prisoners, instead of that humane treatment which those taken by the Continental Army experienced, were in general treated with the greatest barbarity. Many of them were kept nearly five days absolutely without food; and when they received a supply, it was both insufficient in quantity, and of the worst quality. They suffered the utmost distress from cold, nakedness, and close confinement. Freemen, and men of substance, suffered all that a generous mind could suffer, from the contempt and mockery of British and foreign mercenaries. Multitudes died in prison; nor was any charitable assistance afforded to the sick and dying, a neglect which was probably never known to happen, in a similar case, among Christians. The prisoners captured by Sir William Howe, in 1776 amounted to many hundreds, who were shut up, in the coldest season of the year, in churches, sugar-houses, and other large buildings. Many hundreds of these unhappy men expired from the severity of the weather and the rigor of their treatment. The filth of their places of confinement was both offensive and dangerous; and seven dead bodies have been seen in one building, at one time, all lying in a situation shocking to humanity. When those who survived were ordered to be sent out for exchange, some of them fell dead in the streets, while attempting to walk to the vessels, and others were so emaciated that their appearance was horrible. More than eleven thousand persons died on board the Jersey prison-ship, near New York; and for some time after the war the bones of many of these victims lay whitening in the sun on the shores of Long Island. Cunningham, the provost-marshal at New York, it is recorded, as a trait of his villainy, that in the evening he would traverse his domain with a whip in his hand, with the exclamation of "kennel, ye sons of b-----s! Kennel God D--n ye!" Cunningham chose to treat the prisoners like dogs, or worse. (Sanderson 157)

William Cunningham knew that Richard Stockton was a high prize for the British as a signer of the Declaration of Independence, so he would be spared the gallows for now. After a few days, Cunningham decided that Richard Stockton might be used to the advantage of the British General William Howe.

On the day Richard was captured, November 30th, General William Howe and his brother Admiral Richard Lord Howe had written a Proclamation in New York. They wanted to entice the rebels to come back to the king's side. The Proclamation required little of the rebels. Pardon was available to any colonist who would:

"testify his obedience to the laws, by subscribing a declaration in the words following: 'I, _____ do promise and declare, that I will remain in a peaceable obedience to his Majesty, and will not take up arms, nor encourage others to take up arms, in opposition to his authority shall and may obtain a full and free pardon of all treasons and misprisions of treasons, by him heretofore committed or done, and of all forfeitures, attainders, and penalties for the same; and upon producing to us, or to either of us, a certificate of such his appearance and declaration, shall and may have and receive such pardon made and passed to him in due form."

One was not required to swear allegiance to the king, only to remain in peaceable obedience. After agreeing to this Proclamation, one was given "protection papers." Rebels were given only 60 days to take this protection.

To the colonists this pardon was nothing more than a temporary paper that could be forgotten as soon as the enemy had gone. This protection paper when shown to the British and Hessian troops was meant to protect private property, however, this didn't work very well, as the protection paper was ignored and property was looted anyway. Many colonists (4,836) took advantage of this Proclamation in the first few months of the war when things were going badly for Washington and his men. (Gruber 195)

When the British officers and men, and especially the British Parliament found out about the Howes' Proclamation, they were furious. They felt no such protection should be given to these damn rebels and felt the Howes had overstepped their authority to authorize such a Proclamation. The Howe brothers felt it was a good way to win the war with less bloodshed.

If Richard Stockton would agree to accept a pardon for his treasonable offenses against the king and take his protection under Howe's Proclamation, Cunningham thought he would be generously rewarded by General Howe. Howe in turn, could show Parliament, his British countrymen, and his officers that a leading rebel, Richard Stockton, a member of Congress, and a signer of the Declaration of Independence had taken his protection. This outcome would surely appease the criticism of Howe by his British countrymen.

Richard was asked by Cunningham in early December to take his oath under Howe's Proclamation and take the protection. Cunningham hadn't informed General Howe that they held Stockton, as Howe was down in New Jersey chasing General Washington and didn't return until almost Christmas. Cunningham's plan was to have Stockton agree to take protection under the Proclamation, then present him to Howe.

However, Judge Richard Stockton was a man of honor, and his word would not be broken by an offer to take Howe's Protection and admit to treasonable offenses. As a signer of the Declaration of Independence, Richard Stockton had sworn to support that document with his life, his fortune and his sacred honor.

Cunningham was livid! Who was this damn rebel to turn down such an offer of leniency? He would certainly agree to Howe's Proclamation if Cunningham made things worse for him! The officers were told to be especially brutal in their treatment of Richard Stockton. He was afforded no comforts, as he should have been as a man of high standing and station; this was in stark contrast to the treatment of British officers held as prisoners by our Continental army. They were allowed on their parole of honor to live in houses and were provided money for their food and lodging. They were never treated as common criminals as was Stockton.

Cunningham and his British captors did all they could to taunt and humiliate Richard. They told him that General Washington had tucked his tail like a dog and run away from the British army. They delighted in telling him that Washington was a coward, and was unfit to lead any army. They constantly questioned Richard about plans of Congress, where other signers lived, and wanted to know about General Washington's plans for his Continental army. Richard would not give them the information they demanded. So he was subject to brutal beatings then thrown in the dungeon. The worst torment Richard was subjected to, was not the irons on his wrists and ankles, the starvation, the beatings, or the dungeon, but being told that he would be hung, drawn and quartered before the very eyes of his wife and children, that his land and property would be taken by the British, that his family would be left destitute, and that as a traitor to the King, he deserved this and more.

In his travels to England and Scotland in 1766, he had learned of the barbarous treatment of Scottish prisoners by the British after the battle of Culloden in Scotland only 20 years before, and knew what they were capable of. After the defeat of Bonnie Prince Charles Stuart, the Scottish prisoners were put to the sword after they had surrendered. The Scottish leaders of the rebellion were considered traitors to the king, and his British captors delighted in telling him the horrific details the traitors suffered before death. This grotesque means of torture was first used by the British on the Scottish Hero Sir William Wallace (Braveheart, as he would be later known) in 1305. They told Richard he would be hung by the neck but cut down while still alive, then put on a rack with his hands tied to one end and his feet tied to the other and he would be stretched or drawn out. Then his abdomen would be cut open and his bowels

descriptive torture

would be pulled out and burned before his very eyes and his beating heart would then be cut out. He would then be beheaded and his body would be cut in quarters and sent to different areas of the country and displayed as a warning to other traitors. Richard found it hard to understand how anyone could be capable of such cruelty to their fellow man.

Richard recalled his good friend Reverend John Witherspoon telling him of his imprisonment as a young man in his native Scotland. Witherspoon said after the battle of Falkirk in 1746, he as a bystander, was captured and taken to Doune Castle by the Scottish rebels. The prisoners were held in a high tower, and after some thought they decided to fashion a rope from blankets to climb down and make their escape into the night. Several did climb down but before Witherspoon's turn the rope broke and one prisoner was badly injured as he fell to the ground. Witherspoon prudently declined the dangerous attempt to climb down, and patiently awaited his liberation in a safer manner and was released a short time later. Had Witherspoon been treated with the same brutal treatment as Stockton now in the hands of the British - no doubt he would have taken his chance with the broken rope. (Sanderson 209)

As the days torturously passed by, the movement of the irons on his wrists and ankles had bruised and rubbed the skin raw, and now the wounds began to become red and fester. The straw that he laid upon was alive with vermin. Lice now covered his body and rats were everywhere searching for a scrap of food and sometimes becoming a welcome meal for a prisoner lucky enough to catch one. A bucket was kept for the men to relieve themselves, but most of the sick and dying prisoners didn't have the strength to make it to the bucket.

The smell of death was everywhere, and the sight and sounds of the dead and dying would haunt Richard Stockton the rest of his life. The nights held unspeakable horror as the dying men swore, cried out in despair, moaned until mercifully death took them. When he could, Richard tried to bring comfort to the dying, if it was only to put his hand on their arm and tell them they would soon be in a better place, and their country would always remember their sacrifice. Every morning Richard and the other prisoners were made to carry the dead from their cells, and when not confined to the dungeon, he was made to load their emaciated bodies on wagons to be buried in mass graves near the bay. He lost count of the staggering number of prisoners that died in Provost Prison.

Hundreds left names and records carved on the walls. The starving prisoners ate mice, rats and insects - anything to suppress the hunger. For days he would get nothing to eat; then a few weevil infested hard biscuits, twice a week a bit of rancid pork, sometimes eaten raw if there was no firewood, a bit of watered broth from time to time, just enough to keep him alive. The food was as vile as the smell of the prison but he had to eat it or starve.

Old shoes, when worn into the prison by a new prisoner, were torn apart and eaten with as much relish as pork or turkey; and a beef bone of four or five ounces after it was picked clean would be sold by the British guard for soup broth. Many of the prisoners complained they were treated worse than cattle or hogs; at least the animals were well fed. The hours slowly passed to days, weeks, and then stretched into a month, then five weeks. His once fit body now showed the ravages of his brutal treatment. His ribs protruded and the skin now hung on his bones. He could barely walk to the bucket to relieve himself.

Richard's health began to fail him, and he was taken with a fever. Anyone that spent time in a jail, prison or prison ship during the Revolutionary War soon learned it was a death trap. If you didn't starve or freeze to death, sooner or later sickness would raise its ugly head. Smallpox, yellow fever, typhoid fever, the fluxes, dysentery all ran rampant because of the horrid, unsanitary conditions. Smallpox and the fevers had taken many prisoners younger and stronger than he was.

The only respite from this hell for Richard was sleep, with sweet dreams of his family and home. If he was released, and lived through this ordeal, he knew it would take a long time to rebuild his home and law practice so he could again provide for his family. Only his determination to see Annis and the children would keep him alive. It was a time that truly tried his body and soul.

In Fort Greene Park, Brooklyn stands a Prison Martyrs' Monument erected in 1908. Underneath the monument are buried the piles of bones of thousands of American prisoners that for many years after the Revolution were cast up by the tides on the shores of Wallabout Bay in Brooklyn. (Hallahan 245)

American Revolutionary war hero and prisoner of Provost prison Ethan Allen wrote:

> The prisoners who were brought to New York were crowded into churches, and environed with slavish Hessian guards, a people of strange language and at other times by merciless Britons, whose mode of communicating ideas being unintelligible in this country served only to tantalize and insult the helpless and perishing; but above all the hellish delight and triumph of the tories over them, as they were dying by hundreds. This was too much for me to bear as a spectator; for I saw the tories exulting over the dead bodies of their countrymen. I have gone into the churches and seen sundry of the prisoners in the agonies of death, in consequence of very hunger; and others speechless and near death, biting pieces of wood chips; others pleading, for God's sake for something to eat, and at the same time shivering with the cold. Hollow groans saluted my ears, and despair seemed to be imprinted on every of their countenances. The filth in these churches, in consequence of the fluxes, was almost beyond description. I have carefully sought to direct my steps so as to avoid it, but could not. The provisions dealt out to the prisoners was by no means sufficient for the support of life. They would beg for God's sake for one morsel of bread. I have seen in one

of the churches seven dead, at the same time, lying among the excrements of their bodies.

Ethan Allen, later paroled by General Howe, went on to write:

I was in one of the prison yards and a large-boned, tall young man, from Pennsylvania, approached who was reduced to a mere skeleton. He said he was glad to see me before he died, which he had expected to have done last night, but was a little revived. He further informed me that he and his brother had been urged to enlist into the British army, but had died in consequence of that resolve, and that he expected shortly to follow him; but I made the other prisoners stand a little off and told him with a low voice to enlist; he then asked whether it was right in the sight of God? I assured him that it was, and that duty to himself obliged him to deceive the British by enlisting and deserting at the first opportunity; upon which he answered with transport that he would enlist. I charged him not to mention my name as his adviser, lest it could get air and I should be closely confined, in consequence of it.

In times such as this a man sometimes must swallow his pride to live.

During the long weeks of his imprisonment, Richard had time to think about his life, and he questioned whether this cause of Independence was worth the suffering he had endured. He thought about the times his life had been spared by divine intervention, and he always thought God had saved him for a greater cause. Richard sincerely felt that by signing the Declaration of Independence and declaring freedom from Britain and its tyranny, freedom, once acquired, would mean that Annis, his children, his descendents and countrymen would live in a free country, and that it would be worth all his suffering and sacrifices.

Cunningham and the British officers constantly taunted...... Agree to the Proclamation and go home a free man. He could not bring himself to betray his sacred honor; he was a man of his word. Richard knew Annis would get word to Congress of his brutal capture, but he also realized he could not survive much longer, and his only hope was to be paroled or exchanged soon, or he would surely die in this horrible prison.

When new prisoners arrived, the other prisoners made sure that Richard got to talk to them and was informed about the state of the Continental army. The war was not going well, and he was told the army was dissolving fast. Many of the soldiers enlistments had expired on December 1, and over 2,000 refused to sign on again. Others' enlistments were up January 1, and few men were willing to stay on after their obligations expired. Given the conditions they lived under, who could blame them? Many were shoeless and tied rags around their feet and, as General Heath remarked after seeing General Lee's troops pass by, were "so destitute of shoes that the blood left on the frozen ground, in many places, marked the route they had taken." (McCullough 230)

Richard learned from another newly captured officer who had been with his good friend Adjutant-General Joseph Reed that Reed had in desperation written a letter to Washington on December 22, 1776:

> Will it not be possible, my dear General, for our troops or such part of them as can act with advantage to make a diversion or something more at Trenton? The greater the alarm, the more likely success will attend the attacks…I will not disguise my own sentiments that our cause is desperate and hopeless if we do not take the opportunity of the collection of troops at present to strike some stroke. Our affairs are hastening fast to ruin if we do not retrieve them by some happy event. Delay with us is now equal to total defeat. And most of the officers had agreed with Reed. (McCullough 271)

Hundreds had deserted and others that stayed on were hungry, sick and generally miserable. The men were justly dispirited, and some had not been paid for months. General Washington himself was desperate as he wrote to Lund Washington, "Our only dependence now is upon the speedy enlistment of a new army and if this fails, I think the game is pretty near up." (McCullough 207)

Richard was told that new recruits could not be found in New England, the middle colonies or in the South. Washington would soon have to depend solely upon the militia, and the militia was sometimes unwilling to face the British army. In Virginia, no one would enlist even when a twelve pound bounty was offered. In New Jersey few turned out, and in Pennsylvania those coming forward delayed as long as possible. He had heard that many members of Congress were near desperation, inflation was ruining Congress's credit and the Continental currency was nearly worthless. This economic news worried Richard a great deal because, as a member of Congress, and a patriot he had purchased large amounts of Continental currency.

In his fifth week of captivity Richard saw the first spark of hope. Prisoners captured at the battle of Princeton told how, on Christmas Day, General George Washington, had at great odds crossed the ice filled Delaware, taken Trenton and captured over a thousand Hessian prisoners. Richard thought possibly Reed's letter had moved Washington to make that much needed strike at the British.

One young officer told Richard that the well known artist Charles Willson Peale had told him on the morning of the attack on Trenton on Christmas day, that the men looked so wretched that as one of the men had passed by, "he was in an old dirty blanket jacket, his beard long, and his face so full of sores that he could not clean it." The man was so disfigured that Peale had failed at first to recognize that the man was his own brother, James Peale. Such was the sad condition of the Continental Army. (McCullough 263)

Nine days later on January 3, 1777 Washington won the battle of Princeton:

The British army had reportedly butchered many an unresisting prisoner after the battle, and it was of the general opinion that the enemy, the day before, had determined to give no quarter. Many wounded and disabled officers were barbarously mangled, or put to death. A young American soldier was killed by the British cavalry and his body so cruelly hacked and mangled by their sabers that General Washington thought proper to send the body to the British for inspection: it was carried to the post of Sir George Osborne, who simply returned for answer, that he was "no coroner." Such was the treatment of prisoners, and the inhumanity of the enemy.

(Sanderson 158)

A few Continental soldiers were spared by the British when captured, and put in Provost Prison with Richard. One of the captured soldiers told Richard that on December 31, 1776, Washington had made a remarkable appeal to his veteran troops to stay with him. Washington called the regiment into formation and, astride his horse, asked those who would remain to step forward. He offered the men ten dollars bounty for any that would stay another six months, as their enlistments were to expire on that very day. Drums rolled, but no one stepped forward. Minutes passed then Washington turned his horse around and spoke again:

PRISONERS IN THE REVOLUTIONARY WAR BY JOHN TRUMBULL
Charles Allen Munn Collection
Fordham University Library
Bronx, New York

"My brave fellows, you have done all I asked you to do, and more than could be reasonably expected, but your country is at stake, your wives, your houses, and all that you hold dear. You have worn yourselves out with fatigues and hardships, but we know not how to spare you. If you will consent to stay one month longer, you will render that service to the cause of liberty, and to your country, which you can probably never do under any other circumstance." The drums sounded again and the men began to step forward. (McCullough 285)

Many of the prisoners listening to the soldier tell of this glorious moment cried tears of joy for their brave and gallant countrymen, and above all, it gave them hope. Richard was elated by the good news that General Washington and the Continental army were finally turning the tide against the British, and that small spark of hope had now become a flame that caused the British to think maybe this rag-tag group of rebels might have a chance for freedom after all.

The stunning blows to the British in December and January filled General Howe and his men with gloom and despair about the outcome of the war. General Howe's only high point of the month of December was when he learned on his return to New York near Christmas, that he had been knighted by the king for his victory on Long Island and he was now General Sir William Howe.

British General Sir William Howe received in mid January a letter from General George Washington inquiring about the status and condition of Richard Stockton. Washington had been directed by Congress to protest against the treatment of the honorable Richard Stockton of New Jersey, a member of Congress.

FRIDAY, JANUARY 3RD, 1777

Whereas congress hath received information that the honourable Richard Stockton, of New Jersey, and a member of this congress, hath been made a prisoner by the enemy, and that he hath been ignominiously thrown into a common gaol, and there detained:

Resolved, that general Washington be directed to make immediate inquiry into the truth of this report, and if he finds reason to believe it well founded, that he send a flag to general Howe remonstrating against this departure from that humane procedure which has marked the conduct of these states to prisoners who have fallen into their hands; and to know of general Howe whether he chooses this shall be the future rule for treating all such, on both sides, as the fortune of war may place in the hands of either party.

John Hancock then wrote to the Executive Committee of Congress: "January 6, 1777, Howe's treatment of Mr. Stockton is to the last degree shocking and inhuman if report is to be depended on; and the congress have paid attention to it, that they have thought proper to direct General Washington to inquire into the matter." (Letters of Continental Congress, American Archives)

George Washington wrote letters to General Howe about treatment of prisoners:

I would beg that some certain Rule of Conduct towards Prisoners may be settled; if you are determined to make Captivity as distressing as possible, to those whose Lot it is to fall into it, let me know it, that we may be upon equal terms, for your Conduct must and shall mark mine.

If a real scarcity of the Articles of Provision and fuel, at this inclement Season, is the Cause that our prisoners are debarred them, common humanity points out a mode; which is, of suffering them to go home under parole, not to serve during the War, or until an equal number are released by us for them. I am etc. (Writings of George Washington)

General Washington again wrote to Howe:

January 13, 1777

My Lord: I am sorry that I am under disagreeable necessity of troubling your Lordship with a Letter, almost wholly on the subject of the cruel Treatment, -- From the Opinion I have ever been taught to entertain of your Lordship's Humanity, I will not suppose, that you are privy to proceedings of so cruel and unjustifiable a nature; and I hope that, upon making the proper Inquiry, you will have the matter so regulated, that the unhappy Creatures, whose Lot is Captivity, any not in the future have the Miseries of Cold, disease and Famine, added to their other Misfortunes. You may call us Rebels, and say, that we deserve no better treatment; But remember my Lord, that supposing us Rebels, we still have feelings equally as keen and sensible, as Loyalists, and will, if forced to it, most assuredly retaliate upon those, upon whom we look, as the unjust invaders of our Rights, Liberties and properties.

I should not have said thus much, but my injured Countrymen have long called upon me to endeavor to obtain a redress of their Grievances; and I shall think myself as culpable, as those who inflict such severities upon them, were I to continue silent.

There are two Captains of Merchantmen by the Name of Bell and Getshius on Board the Whitley prison Ship; if your Lordship will grant them their Liberty upon Parole, I will engage to send two British Masters in Exchange for them. I am etc.

When General Sir William Howe, now back in New York and staying busy with his mistress, Mrs. Loring and the turning tide of battles received the letter from General George Washington in mid January, he called for his provost marshal William Cunningham. When Cunningham arrived, Howe inquired about Richard Stockton and was told that indeed Stockton was held by the British and was in Provost Prison in New York just a few miles away. Howe asked Cunningham to bring Richard Stockton to him at once.

Cunningham was now concerned that he might be in serious trouble with Howe because he had kept Stockton in such horrid conditions and treated him in such a brutal way. Cunningham rushed back to the prison and instructed that Stockton's irons be removed and that Stockton should be brought under guard to his home a short distance from the prison.

When Stockton arrived, Cunningham took him into his kitchen

SIR WILLIAM HOWE
Commander in Chief of his
Majesty's Forces in America

where he had instructed his housekeeper to prepare hot water for a bath. Stockton was left in the kitchen with a guard present so he could bathe. This was the first time Richard had been allowed to wash himself in nearly six weeks. He made good use of the harsh soap and scrubbed his hair, scalp and body to try and rid himself of the lice that covered him.

The guard handed him some clean clothing to put on and his filthy, and vermin infested nightshirt and breeches were burned in the nearby fire. The housekeeper appeared and served him some bread and soup, and as he sat in the kitchen near the warm fire he finally felt like a human being for the first time in a very long time. Cunningham strode into the kitchen, then wheeled around to face Richard and in no uncertain terms told Richard, if he knew what was good for him, he had better keep his mouth shut about the treatment he had received in the Provost Prison.

Since Richard was in no condition to walk any distance, Cunningham called for a carriage to take them the few miles to General Howe's home that he shared with Mrs. Loring. An aid to the General met them at the door and escorted Cunningham and Stockton to the parlor.

Richard Stockton, weak, barely able to walk and sick with fever, now stood before Howe in the first clean and descent clothing he had worn in six weeks. He was a pitiful figure of the man he had been just six weeks earlier. Howe, seated in a chair in the parlor, looked up and was clearly shocked by the emaciated condition of Stockton. Cunningham was promptly dismissed from the room, and told to wait in the kitchen where some of Howe's aides were gambling.

General Howe stood and motioned to a nearby chair provided for Stockton. Stockton remained standing as Howe inquired about Stockton's treatment while held by Cunningham. Richard was not persuaded by Cunningham's threat to keep quiet. Now was the time to let the General know how his provost was treating the prisoners under his command. He owed it to himself and the other prisoners now living and dead, to bring the atrocities he suffered under Cunningham and his men to the attention of General Howe. Howe seemed stunned as Stockton poured out the past six weeks of horror that he spent at the hands of Cunningham and his men. He showed Howe the raw sores on his wrists and ankles caused by the irons he was forced to wear, and opened his shirt to show his protruding ribs and the sunken gaunt frame of his body that was only six weeks ago the same size as Howe's. Howe was speechless, as Stockton finished then sank into the chair Howe had provided for him, totally exhausted. General Howe was a noble and a gentleman, and he wanted to make amends to Stockton for his treatment while in British custody. He had not wanted this war and had even once sworn not to fight against his Colonial brothers. He tried to spare bloodshed by writing the Proclamation now being taken by so many colonists in New York, New Jersey and other states.

Howe offered Richard Stockton his freedom if he would agree to his Proclamation to cease and desist from treasonable actings and remain in peaceable obedience to his majesty. By doing so he would receive protection papers and a full pardon. Stockton refused the offer, stating that he could have agreed to the Proclamation more than a month before when it was first offered to him by Cunningham. As an Honorable man, he could not agree to the Proclamation, as he had signed the Declaration of Independence, pledged his Sacred Honor to uphold it, and could not accept a pardon admitting treason.

Howe understood, as he was also a man of high station and honor, even if he was on the opposite side of this war, and he admired Stockton for his bravery. As an officer and gentleman General Howe was truly sorry for Richard's brutal treatment and told him so. Howe then offered Stockton his freedom on a parole if he would sign a declaration, and give his word of honor that he would no longer participate in the war or meddle in American affairs, as was required of anyone that took a parole on either side. (American Archives, V3: 1604)

As sick as he was, Richard being an excellent lawyer considered his options. He had not been taken in arms; therefore he probably could not be exchanged for a British prisoner of war. As a member of Congress he was considered a traitor to the King after he signed the Declaration of

Independence, and if he did not take a parole at this time, he would probably die if he went back to prison. If he didn't die in prison, he would surely be convicted of high treason and hung, drawn and quartered as a deterrent to others, especially after Cunningham learned he had told Howe about his brutal treatment. As soon as Howe left New York, Richard knew that Cunningham could do as he pleased with the prisoners again.

At this point in time Richard had sacrificed his health; he was extremely sick, probably near death and had suffered dreadfully for his country, and his family needed him. He was too sick to participate in the war, so he did the only thing he could to save his life. After six weeks of hell in Provost Prison, and under much duress he signed Howe's declaration, giving his word of honor that he would not meddle in American affairs during the war, and was given his parole by Howe. He knew taking a parole was an honorable thing to do, and there was no shame in it. The Continental army gave paroles to thousands of British and Hessian officers and soldiers. It was a common practice on both sides in this revolutionary war.

He was proud to have been a signer of the Declaration of Independence, and he would never renounce it publicly or privately, or ever support the King and his British army; he was no turncoat and he did not sign Howe's Proclamation. His time in prison had been brutal, and he felt fortunate to be alive when so many others had died in that horrible prison. He would never forget his fellow prisoners, and their suffering and sacrifices for their country would haunt him for the rest of his life. Richard hoped his words to General Howe about the treatment of his fellow prisoners would bring about some marked improvements to their conditions.

Ethan Allen as a prisoner in Provost prison in late 1776 wrote: "Our little army was retreating in New Jersey and our young men murdered by hundreds in New York." He speaks of Washington's success at Trenton and Princeton in the following terms:

> This success had a mighty effect on General Howe and his council, and roused them to a sense of their own weakness. The prisoners, who were condemned to the most wretched and cruelest of deaths, and who survived to this period, though most of them died before, were immediately ordered to be sent within General Washington's lines, for an exchange, and in consequence of it were taken out of their filthy and poisonous places of confinement, and sent out of New York to their friends in haste. Several of them fell dead in the the streets of New York, as they attempted to walk to the vessels in the harbor, for their intended embarkation. What number lived to reach the lines I cannot ascertain, but, I apprehend that most of them died in consequence of the vile usage of the enemy.

And he further wrote:

> Upon the best calculation I have been able to make from personal knowledge, and the many evidences I have

collected in support of the facts, I learn that, of the prisoners taken on Long Island and Fort Washington and some few others, at different times and places, about two thousand perished with hunger, cold, and sickness, occasioned by the filth of their prisons, at New York.
(Dandridge Chapter XII)

General Howe, remorseful after hearing of the cruel and brutal treatment dealt to Richard Stockton at the hands of Cunningham, decided to parole and exchange prisoners in order to save their lives, showing his compassion as a high ranking British officer. And saving the lives of hundreds of prisoners as a result.

A London journal gave the British account of American prisoners: "Jan 14, 1777; The churches are full of American prisoners who die so fast we bury 25-30 at a time. General Howe gave all who could walk their liberty, after taking their oath not to take up arms." (Dandridge Chapter XII)

General Howe gave Stockton a bed for the night and the next morning after breakfast he was brought a horse to ride home, a warm coat and some food for his journey. General Howe told Richard that he hoped to see him again when this awful war was over and wished him well. For the first time in what seemed like a lifetime Richard felt that he would live to see his family again.

General Sir William Howe wrote to Lord Germain in England on March 25, 1777 that 4,836 colonists had taken his protection, but at no time had a leading rebel sought pardon. Taking Howe's Proclamation, receiving protection papers and a pardon differed greatly from signing a declaration and receiving a parole. Richard Stockton's steadfast refusal to accept Howe's Proclamation, take protection and a pardon had given Howe no leading rebel to write home about.

After an arduous two day journey, Richard was able to track his family to the home of his sister Hanna and brother-in-law Elias Boudinot, now residing at their farm in nearby Basking Ridge, New Jersey. He was at long last united with his joyful wife Annis and their children. Everyone was clearly shocked by his gaunt appearance. He learned that Benjamin, Julia, and John Richard were all safe. He felt he had truly been blessed. Elias, appointed by General George Washington to be the commissary general of prisoners, told Richard that on the very day he had been captured November 30, he had been elected to another term in Congress:

At a joint meeting of the Council and Assembly of the State of New Jersey, held at Burlington, on the 30th day of November, 1776, the Honourable Nathaniel Scudder in the chair; the joint meeting proceeded by ballot to the election of five Delegates, to represent this State in Congress, to serve for one year, unless a new appointment should be made before the expiration of that time; and the following persons were duly elected, viz; The Honourable Richard Stockton, Jonathan Dickinson Sergeant, Esq., Dr.

John Witherspoon, Abraham Clarke, Esq., Jonathan Elmer, Esq.

Resolved, That any one or more of the said Delegates, who shall attend in Congress, be fully empowered to represent, and vote in behalf of this State. That the said Delegates, or such of them as have not already taken the oaths of abjuration and allegiance mentioned in the act of Assembly lately passed, entitled An Act for the Security of the Government of New Jersey, do take the said oaths before they take their seats.

Signed by order of the Council and Assembly of the State of New Jersey, Charles Pettit, Secretary. (American Archives Documents of the American Revolution 1774-1776)

Because of the parole he signed to gain his freedom and his agreement not to participate in the war in addition to his terrible state of health Richard sat down and wrote a letter of resignation to Congress.

Elias told Richard that Congress, now located in Baltimore, had only 20 members present according to John Adams, and Adams had implored Thomas Jefferson and others to return and aid the country.

In Pennsylvania the regular assembly was disputing efforts by the revolutionary convention to levy taxes; in New Jersey bands of loyalists declared themselves ready to fight alongside the king's army and in Virginia patriots became less ardent as the victories of Howe's army became known. New York City and adjoining counties petitioned the Howes, and asked to be declared at peace; revolutionary committees near New York dissolved themselves, disclaimed the authority of Congress, and repudiated their former actions; and militia in Westchester County and on Long Island had signified their willingness to fight alongside the British army. (Gruber 198)

The winter of 1776 George Washington and the Continental Army made camp in Morristown, New Jersey. Elias Boudinot and family resided in nearby Basking Ridge. Little Susan Boudinot was at times a victim of nerves. One day hearing target practice, she flew home crying, "The British are coming! The British are coming!" Martha Washington, who happened to be visiting caught her in her arms and reassured her. (Boyd 84)

Such was the turmoil in this country in the early months of the Revolutionary war. Richard Stockton had served his country with dignity. Now he would try to rebuild his life. He needed to go home and take care of himself and his young family. He had given much to the cause of freedom and was fortunate to have survived. He rested a few days trying to regain his strength. At first he could only manage a little broth and bread, but his appetite was returning, his fever seemed better, and he was growing stronger by the day.

His family would be his best medicine, and they were grateful to have their loving father and husband back with them. They were crowded in the house with many others seeking refuge with Elias and Hanna, but thankful to have a warm place to stay and food to eat.

A week went by before Annis and Richard traveled by coach to Morven to be united with John Richard and their trusted servant, Samuel. John Richard was distressed that he was not able to keep their home safe from the plunder of the British army. Richard told him they were proud of his effort and were thankful to be with their brave young son at last.

While in Princeton in late January, they met with their son-in-law Benjamin Rush. Rush wrote, "At Princeton I met my wife's father who had been plundered of all his household furniture and stock by the British army, and carried a prisoner to New York, from whence he was permitted to return to his family upon parole." (Corner 130)

Rush later wrote: "The whole of Mr. Stockton's furniture, apparel, and even valuable writings have been burnt. All his cattle, horses, hogs, sheep, grain and forage have been carried away by them. His losses cannot amount to less than five thousand pounds." (*Letters of Benjamin Rush*, Vol. I, 126) This was a fortune at that time.

Richard was devastated by the condition of his home and property.

Morven had been British General Cornwallis's headquarters for his two brief stays at Princeton and the headquarters of Colonel William Harcourt of the Sixteenth Dragoons, who had captured General Charles Lee of the Continental army, near Basking Ridge for the rest of the time Morven was occupied by the British. The furniture, clothes and pictures, had been taken; the wine cellar looted. The east wing had been reduced to blackened walls and charred beams. The papers, family records and the valuable library that it contained, one of the finest in the colonies, had been burned, and forever lost.

The portraits of Richard and Annis were torn from their frames, slashed, then bayoneted and thrown outside. Two of the buried chests of valuables had been revealed to the British by another servant probably under duress, and had been looted. But one had remained hidden and it contained the prized tankard bearing the Stockton coat of arms and their silver. Two of Annis's favorite books, her Bible and Young's *Night Thoughts*, were among the few books salvaged. As she searched among the straw, the soldiers had used to bed down, she found to her delight, some of the letters Richard had written to her during his many absences. (Bill 42)

Their crops were destroyed and all the livestock, including Richard's prized horses, sheep and cattle were all gone.

Richard felt fortunate to have survived his brutal imprisonment, and together he and Annis would hopefully be able to rebuild their home, but it would be a long difficult struggle filled with unfortunate downfalls and heartaches along the way.

Only a month before Princeton had become a ghost town and now people returned cautiously. Everyone was suspicious of their neighbor and rumors and false accusations ran rampant in the small town. This was a time of civil war, as well as a revolutionary war, and it was neighbor against neighbor, brother against brother and in the case of Benjamin Franklin, father against son. William Franklin was now the imprisoned former Royal Governor of New Jersey and a sworn Loyalist while his father, Benjamin Franklin was a signer of the Declaration of Independence and a strong rebel, and they would never heal the break between them as long as they lived.

A rumor about Richard Stockton was spread by a loyalist named Cochran, a sworn enemy of Stockton, saying Stockton had gone over to General Howe and taken his protection and that was the reason he had been in New York. Probably, the rumor took hold, in part, because of confusion between Judge Richard Stockton and his cousin, one Major Richard Stockton. "Common report, moreover, may have attributed to him [Judge Stockton] some of the exploits of a distant cousin, Major Richard Stockton, a particularly obnoxious Tory" who did join the British and was captured by Washington's men at nearly the same time Stockton was paroled. (Bill 43)

For a short time this rumor about Stockton was believed by some, and he was spoken against, but soon people realized it was nothing but a

61

lie, based on mistaken identity and spread by Cochran for malicious reasons. When people realized Judge Richard Stockton had been a prisoner, brutally treated by the British, and paroled by General Howe, the rumor was dismissed by the citizens of Princeton. A parole was given after signing a declaration and giving your word of honor not to take up arms or meddle in affairs of the war. Howe's Proclamation was far more in that it required you remain obedient to the king and accused you of treasonable acts. For signing the Proclamation you were given a pardon of all treasons committed, and given protection papers.

As John Rogers had written to John Witherspoon December 24, 1776 after Richard's capture: "You will find him (Stockton) a Gent [leman] n of Genuis {sic} & Learning, & you may assuredly depend upon his Intelligence as a Person of the strictest Probity (honesty)." (Gerlach 338) Gerlach further writes: "Brutal treatment in a British prison prevented this signer of the Declaration of Independence from participating in the political life of the new nation." (104)

The townspeople were not long forgetful of the services and sacrifices Richard Stockton had rendered to the cause of Independence. General George Washington while in Morristown took the time to issue a general order: "February 3, 1777. Parole Vienna. Countersign Wilmington. Any officers, or soldiers of the American Army, who are possessed of Bonds, or other papers, belonging to Mr. Stockton, are strictly ordered to deliver them to the Adjutant General at Head-Quarters." (The Writings of George Washington from the Original Manuscript Sources, Fitzpatrick) After the battle of Princeton,

troops were allowed to roam around the village, and Washington thought some of them might have picked up valuable documents belonging to Richard. No bonds or papers were ever returned, as they had no doubt fallen into the hands of the enemy when Morven was occupied by General Cornwallis and his men. General Washington's thoughtful treatment of Stockton and the influence he retained in his standing with Continental authorities is further proof that Stockton was under no suspicion of misconduct.

Over 3,500 people in New Jersey had signed Howe's Proclamation and had taken a protection. British General Sir William Howe in March 1777, in a letter to the British Parliament, two months after Stockton's parole wrote: "Joseph Galloway, once speaker of the House of Assembly of Pennsylvania, was the only notable colonist that accepted the Howe Proclamation and no other leading rebel took protection." (Griffith 332) This document provides further proof that Stockton never accepted protection, and the letter was written by the very man who gave Stockton his parole. Galloway, who signed the Proclamation, gave aid to the British army and ended up fleeing to England after the war. General Washington wanted to capture Galloway and hang him as a traitor to his country. Had those rumors been true about Stockton, George Washington certainly would have held him accountable for his actions.

Anyone who crossed enemy lines, even as a prisoner like Richard Stockton was required to take an oath of allegiance to the United States. "Princeton, 1777 December 22, Met pursuant to adjournment. Present – Governor, Mehelm, Smith Imlay, Manning, Mr. Speaker. Richard Stockton Esqr. was called before the Board and took the Oaths and was dismissed." (Council of Safety Minutes, State of New Jersey 1777-1778, 70)

Every man that had taken protection from Howe was required to state his name and turn in the protection papers. The protection papers being turned in were noted in the minutes, and then oath of allegiance was sworn. An example of those turning in protection papers and those that refused:

26 April 1777, Met according to adjournment. Present – Governor, Elmer, Scudder, Patterson, Hart, Combes. Ordered that William Tice and William Smith appear before the Board, both examined again, heard and dismissed on taking of the Oaths. Daniel Hendrickson, who was summoned as a person suspected of being disaffected and dangerous attended, was examined, and acknowledged that he had received a Protection from the Enemy which he refused to give up when demanded by the Board. Oaths were tendered and he refused to take them but was ready with his surety Edward Taylor Esqr. at 300 pounds to enter into recognizance to appear at the next Court of General Quarter Sessions of the Peace of Monmouth County, was told to be of good behavior and was dismissed. Abraham Smith and Isaac Sharp of Monmouth appeared, were examined, delivered up their Protection, took the Oaths and were dismissed. (Council of Safety Minutes, State of New Jersey 1777-1778, p. 13)

Richard Stockton had not taken protection from Howe, and did not turn in any protection papers as noted in the minutes of the Council of Safety. Stockton proved he was innocent of the rumor that he had taken protection from Howe.

Only a few months later at Valley Forge, Washington would require all his officers to take the oath of allegiance as there was such widespread doubt of loyalty in this country. The members of Congress from his own state of New Jersey had also been required to take the oath of allegiance before taking their seats in Congress in November, 1776.

Accounts from Philadelphia indicated that some of the foremost members had left Congress after signing the Declaration of Independence and had gone home to take care of their families and business. The three major contributors to the Declaration of Independence were absent. Jefferson had gone home in September, John Adams was home in Braintree, and Benjamin Franklin had set sail for France. Many others were ill, exhausted or absent and there was "much alarm" in the city and in Congress. They had done their duty to their country by signing that immortal document and set the country on its road to freedom. Many members of Congress lost their fortunes, and their lives were forever changed, as in the case of Richard Stockton, but no signer suffered as much as Stockton in the hands of the British.

Signers Edward Rutledge and Thomas Hayward, were captured while defending Charleston, South Carolina in November 1780 and taken to St. Augustine, Florida. Arthur Middleton was captured and released on parole when he was taken prisoner near Charleston a few months earlier, but after Charleston surrendered, he was again taken prisoner and sent along with Rutledge and Hayward to St. Augustine. They were prisoners of the British, but they were not placed in close confinement, treated as common criminals or starved and exposed to freezing weather as was the case with Stockton, according to the accounts in Sanderson's book on the Signers of the Declaration of Independence written in 1823. Nevertheless they suffered as prisoners of war, and were held nearly a year. Hayward and fellow signer George Walton had been wounded earlier fighting the British, and all their plantations were pillaged. After Walton was injured fighting the British in Savannah, Georgia, he was allowed to recuperate under a parole. When he recovered, he was arrested and then exchanged for a British officer. Elizabeth Lewis, the wife of signer Francis Lewis, was captured by the British after their home was plundered in the autumn of 1776, and held prisoner in New York. She was without a bed to lie on and without a change of clothes until Congress was notified on November 8, 1776. General Washington, when advised of the situation had her exchanged for two British officers' wives. (Sanderson 2: 155) Fortunately she was better fed, and not put in irons, but this brave woman lost her health like Stockton, and died two years later.

On February 4, 1778 a year after Richard Stockton's parole, Elias Boudinot, Stockton's brother-in-law and commissary general of prisoners for the Continental army, wrote a Report to General Washington on conditions in New York, and found British Prisons worse than reported:

I waited on General Robertson (Commandant of New

York City in 1778) at breakfast. He behaved as before with the greatest civility and good humor. The General told me that he knew we had heard strange stories within our lines of their conduct to our prisoners, and said that as a gentleman I should go as I pleased to inspect the prisons and that I would find the charges a parcel of damned lies. I asked to be accompanied by a British officer so that I should not see a prisoner but in the presence of the officer attending me. He agreed to the proposal, observing again that he was sure I should find the reports we had heard totally false....Accordingly I went to a Prison with the officer, Mr. Loring, where we found near 30 officers, from colonels downwards, in close confinement. After some conversation with Ethan Allen, I told him my errand, on which he was very free in his abuse of the British on account of the cruel treatment he had received during his months of close confinement. I had the officers drawn up in a ring and informed them of my mission. That my design was to obtain them the proper redress, but if they kept back anything from an improper fear of their keepers, they would have themselves only to blame for their want of redress. On some hesitation from a dread of their keeper, the Provost Marshal, one of them began and informed us that they had been confined on the most frivolous pretenses. That they had received the most cruel treatment from the Provost Marshal, being locked up in the dungeon on the most trifling pretenses, such as asking for water on a hotter day than usual. Some of them were kept 10, 12, 14 weeks in the dungeon. Their drinking water would be brought back in the same tubs they had to use to relieve themselves in, and they must drink it or perish. After hearing a number of the instances of extreme cruelty, I asked who the person responsible was. They answered 'the provost keeper.' He accordingly came in, and on being informed of what had passed, I asked if the complaints were true. He with great insolence answered that every word was true—on which the British officer, abusing him very much, asked him how he dared to treat gentlemen in that cruel manner. He, insolently putting his hands to his side, swore that he was as absolute there as General Howe was at the head of his army. I observed to the officer, Mr. Loring, that now there could be no dispute about facts as the fellow had acknowledged every word to be true....at Provost Prison Elias observed .....

I was greatly distressed with the wretched situation of so many of the human species. That on meeting all the prisoners of war together in a room, in company with Mr. Loring, I heard their complaints and took notes of the accusations on which they were severally confined. They repeated to me instances of the most shocking barbarity in presence of the keeper of the Provost, whom they charged as the instigator: the beating of officers of rank and distinction on the most trivial occasion, locking them up in the dark damp dungeons for many months. That besides prisoners of war, there are many here, as Committee Men, Commissioners, etc, etc., who are wretched beyond description. That inhabitants and persons in civil departments when taken are sent to the Provost without distinction, and at present there seems to be no redemption for them....I waited on General Robertson, who said he hoped I was quite satisfied of the falsity of the reports I had heard..... I stated to him the facts and assured him that they turned out worse than anything we had heard. The British officer with me, Mr. Loring, confirmed the facts and General Robertson expressed great dissatisfaction, and on stating the case of each of these unhappy men, he very humanely agreed to the discharge of all the officers (except seven) on their parole; and gave me the strongest assurances that he would not again allow of such a power on the sergeant of the Provost, and promised the Provost Marshal would be punished. (Commager and Morris 865)

It seems things had not changed since Stockton was imprisoned in New York. The British officers were either not aware of the atrocities committed by Cunningham, Loring and others on the unfortunate prisoners, or looked the other way until Elias Boudinot or Washington brought it to their attention, and then they took action.

Nearly two thousand helpless American prisoners were slowly starved, frozen, or poisoned in the churches and other prisons in New York. This does not include the 11,000 prisoners that died on the infamous prison ships harbored in New York.

We attempt to give some idea of the horrors of their hopeless captivity. Anyone who endured imprisonment for any length of time in the churches and prisons of New York was fortunate to live to tell the tale. One of these churches was standing not many years ago, and the marks of bayonet thrusts might plainly be seen upon its pillars. What terrible deeds were enacted there we can only conjecture. We know that two thousand, healthy, high-spirited young men, many of them sons of gentlemen, and all patriotic, brave, and long enduring, even unto death, were foully murdered in these places of torment. We know, that these young men perished awfully, rather than enlist in the British army; that posterity has almost forgotten them, and that their dreadful sufferings ought to be remembered wherever American history is read. (Dandridge IX)

THE EARLY YEARS

Richard Stockton's great-grandfather, also named Richard, emigrated from Cheshire, England in 1655 and settled in Long Island, near the city of New York. His family were anciently Lords of the Manor of Stockton, in the town of Malpas, near the City of Chester, England. According to a history of the family in the College of Arms in London, the family was located there at the time of the Norman Conquest (1066) and many memorials of the family in the church there, which was the chapel of a religious house of monks in the Monastic ages, indicate the Anglo-Saxon origin of the family. The direct line of the family terminated in a female heir, Isabella Stockton, who married Robert de Eaton and their descendant married Ralph Grosvenor, Esq. and from her the ducal family of Westminster (the Grosvenor family) descends. David Stockton, Esq. the eldest son, inherited Stockton Manor from his father in 1250, and it went through Isabella to the Grosvenor family.

Lieutenant Richard Stockton arrived in America accompanied by his wife and son Richard in 1655 after the death of King Charles I, when a good many of his friends known as the Cavalier Party came over from England. Among these Cavaliers were the ancestors of George Washington and other famous Virginians who were engaged in the American Revolution. One of Stockton's ancestors, Sir John Stockton was knighted on the field of battle by King Edward IV and was Lord Mayor of London in 1470.

Lieutenant Richard Stockton first resided in Flushing, Long Island,

N.Y. and the records of the town show he resided there in 1656 and was a land owner there. He was commissioned a Lieutenant of Horse in 1665 under Royal Government (King Charles II) and was elected Lieutenant of the Foot Company of Flushing in 1669. In 1691 he became a member of the Society of Friends or Quakers as they were known. In 1701 his son Richard Stockton bought 5,500 acres of land from William Penn. The land sits nearly in the center of Princeton, New Jersey. In 1709 he died leaving land to his six sons, and the house and land to the second youngest son John when he came of age.

John Stockton was a man of great respectability and resided on his estate as an independent country gentleman. He fell in love and married his cousin Abigail, and because she was of another faith, John could no longer remain in the Quaker religion. He became a Presbyterian like his wife; and they had a happy marriage that included sons Richard, John, Philip and Samuel, and daughters Hannah, Abigail, Susannah, and Rebecca. He was a liberal friend to the College of New Jersey that would later be known as Princeton University. John Stockton and two other wealthy men of Princeton signed a bond for a thousand pounds to secure its establishment at Priceton. In addition, they gave ten acres of cleared land and two hundred acres of woodland. Plans were drawn for the college building (Nassau Hall) that would be the largest structure in the colonies; on July 29, 1754, the foundation was begun; and in November two years later President Burr and seventy students moved in. (Bill 16) John Stockton presided as chief judge of the court of Common Pleas for many years prior to his death in 1757.

Richard, the signer of the Declaration of Independence, was the oldest son of John Stockton. He was born October 1, 1730 at his family home in Princeton. He was educated in the early years by Rev. Doctor Samuel Finley at an academy in Maryland. He then attended the College of New Jersey at Newark graduating in 1748.

> After he graduated, he applied himself to the study of law under the direction of the honorable David Ogden of Newark, at that time the most eminent lawyer in the providence. He was admitted to the bar in 1754 and to the grade of counselor in 1758. He stood, in fact for many years and by universal consent, unrivalled at the bar among his contemporaries who were men of learning and brilliant talents. He was frequently invited to conduct cases of importance in Pennsylvania, where he acquired the friendship of prominent and distinguished members of the bar. In 1763 he received the degree of Sergeant at law the highest degree of law at that time. When he traveled to England, Scotland and Ireland in 1766, the fame of his high character and distinguished abilities had preceded him, and he was received with flattering attention by the most eminent men of the kingdom. (Sanderson 3: 84)

He had a law office in Newark as well as in Princeton. Among the more notable students he taught were William Paterson, who was to be

Annis Boudinot Stockton

PORTRAIT BY JOHN WOLLASTON
ANNIS BOUDINOT STOCKTON
Princeton University Art Museum
Used by permission
Bequest of Mrs. Alexander T. McGill
Photo Credit: Bruce M. White

a justice of the Supreme Court of the United States, his brother-in-law Elias Boudinot, President of the Continental Congress in 1782, and Adjutant-General Joseph Reed later to become the trusted advisor of General George Washington.

Annis Boudinot was the first daughter born of Catherine Williams and Elias Boudinot in Darby, Pennsylvania, July 1, 1736. Descended from French Huguenots, her grandfather had fled France at the revocation of the Edict of Nantes in 1685 and settled in New York. Her father, as a young man in New York, apprenticed as a silversmith and merchant, then traveled to the West Indies to run a small plantation. There her father married Catherine, the daughter of a Welsh planter in Antigua, West Indies. From Antigua they moved to Darby, Pennsylvania where Annis was born, then on to Philadelphia a few years later where her father established a shop and home next door to Benjamin Franklin. In his shop he worked as a trained silversmith, and repaired clocks. Her father had enrolled his sons John, Elias and Elisha into Franklin's Academy, and in 1752 they moved to New Brunswick, then later on to Princeton. The family lived in a house rented from Rev. Aaron Burr the president of the College of New Jersey. In 1756, they moved to a home opposite Nassau Hall, and her father became Postmaster of Princeton and also opened a tavern.

This brought Annis into the social center of the small town. She became a close friend of Esther and Aaron Burr. Aaron Burr was the minister-president of the College of New Jersey. His wife Esther remarked to a friend "I must tell you what for neighbors I have – the Nighest is a young Lady that lately moved from Brunswick, a pretty discreet well behaved girl. She has good sense and can talk very handsomely on almost any subject." When Esther's sister Lucy visited in May, 1757, Annis tended her when she fell ill with smallpox and it seems Annis contracted the disease and fell ill in June but recovered. It is interesting that George Washington had also fallen victim to smallpox as a young man. Esther and Aaron remained friends with Annis until their untimely deaths from smallpox a few years later, when their young son Aaron was just a small boy. (Mulford 14)

The fact that Annis Stockton could write and that she wrote poems was remarkable. Most women of her class were able to read, even though the only thing they read was the Bible. Some young women could write, if only their names. Young women who could read and write, and wrote poetry were most unusual. What made Annis extraordinary was that she could also do needlework and played the harp.

She was petite, fair skinned, with brown eyes and long dark curly hair that framed her face, a vision of loveliness. It wasn't long before she was noticed by Richard Stockton, a handsome young bachelor and lawyer of 26, and they were soon engaged to be married.

Annis could speak on most subjects, and Richard was smitten with her knowledge, poise and beauty. Most of the ladies he was acquainted with seemed dull compared with the exciting and interesting Miss Annis Boudinot. She was admired by her friends for her writing ability, and some of her poems had been published. Annis Stockton's poems were widely published in newspapers of the day such as *Pennsylvania Chronicle*, the *New York Mercury* and periodicals such as the *Columbian Magazine*, the *New American Magazine* and *American Museum*. Over her lifetime she would write over 120 different works. Her published works and manuscripts gave her a wide audience in the colonies, with international readers as well. "The quality and quantity of Annis Stockton's literary output makes her an apt counterpart to her seventeenth-century predecessor Anne Bradstreet and the nineteenth-century poet Emily Dickinson." (Mulford 1)

Unlike some prominent men of the day, Richard Stockton was unwilling to marry just to move up in position. He would marry for love alone. He and Annis were a perfect match even though she was from a family far less prominent that his. It seems not everyone was pleased with their courtship as Annis wrote: "I found me all thy own in spite of those whose cold unfeeling minds would bid us part." Richard and Annis were married the fall of 1757, and their first daughter Julia was born on March 2, 1759, followed by twins Mary and Susan on April 17, 1761, John Richard April 17, 1764, Lucius Horatio in 1768, and Abigail September 8, 1773.

Life was good for Richard and Annis. Shortly after they married his father died, and he inherited the Stockton land and built the house that Annis named "Morven" after the home of King Fingal, the father of the Gaelic bard Ossian, created by James Macpherson in 1762. Annis kept the estate running smoothly during his many absences. His work as a prominent lawyer took him from his home for long periods of time. They both took pleasure in working in the garden, planting and arranging the many trees and flowers they acquired.

For 10 years after his marriage Richard continued in his lucrative law practice. As for politics he wrote his former student Joseph Reed in 1764, "The public is generally unthankful and I will never become a servant of it, till I am convinced that by neglecting my own affairs, I am doing more acceptable service to God and man." But like his father before, it wasn't long before he would accept his duty to public service. Before his father's death, he had raised funds for the College of New Jersey, and in 1759 he gave an acre of land to be used for the new Presbyterian Church. The college cooperated on the project and took title to the building, which was built on the land and became a College Chapel. He also gave a mortgage for 212 pounds to meet a payment due on college land. He, like his father, would become a trustee for the college for 26 years and serve the college faithfully until his death.

Richard started to acquire property around Princeton due to the revenue from his lucrative law practice and his holdings included the properties known as Red Hill, Denton's Place, and Mount Lucas all bordering Morven. He bought meadowland along Stoney Brook creek and a farm. He also purchased the Sign of the College Inn that would later be known as Nassau Inn that lies in the middle of Princeton today. His holdings were large and also included houses in the town of Princeton.

NASSAU HALL AND
PRESIDENT'S HOUSE IN 1764
Sketch by Kathryn Glynn
from an original drawing by W. Tennent

The Journey across the Ocean

Having gained a sizeable fortune at the age of 36, Richard decided to travel to Europe, and in the years 1766 and 1767, he visited England, Scotland and Ireland. He wanted Annis to accompany him, but she chose to stay in Princeton with their young children fearing for their safety on such a long voyage. In the month of June he left New York and traveled to London. His fame and high character along with his distinguished abilities preceded him, and he was received with flattering attention by the most eminent men of the kingdom. He was presented at the court of St. James by one of the king's ministers, and Richard had the honor of personally presenting to King George III an address of the trustees of the College of New Jersey, acknowledging the repeal of the Stamp Act, and his address was favorably received by the king. The services he rendered to the College of New Jersey on his visit to Great Britain were so numerous that on his return to America he received the formal thanks of the board of trustees.

When Parliament had resolved to raise revenue in the colonies in 1775, Richard had declared that the colonies "must each of them send one or two of their most ingenious fellows, and enable them to get into the House of Commons, and maintain them there till they can maintain themselves, or else we shall be fleeced to some purpose." (Miller 226) While in London, Richard met with Benjamin Franklin and conferred with London merchants on the issue of paper money by the colonies and an act of Parliament forbidding it.

Judge Richard Stockton

PORTRAIT BY JOHN WOLLASTON
RICHARD STOCKTON
Princeton University Art Museum
Used by permission
Bequest of Mrs. Alexander T. McGill
Photo Credit: Bruce M. White

Annis Boudinot Stockton

Princeton University Art Museum
Used by permission
Bequest of Mrs. Alexander T. McGill
Photo Credit: Bruce M. White

Tall and with a commanding presence, he had the carriage of an accomplished swordsman and horseman that he was. His handsome features and dignified and highly polished manners made him very popular. While in London, he attended the Queen's birthday ball. A young Englishwoman, Esther DeBerdt, engaged to Richard's former law student Joseph Reed remarked, "I like Mr. Stockton exceedingly. He is certainly the cleverest man I have yet seen from America, and I take an uncommon pleasure in his company." (Quoted in [William B. Reed], *The Life of Esther DeBerdt*, afterwards Esther Reed (Philadelphia 1853, 97)

He was consulted on the state of American affairs by such notable men as the Marquis of Rockingham with whom he spent a week at his country estate in Yorkshire. He met with the Earl of Chatham as well as other distinguished members of Parliament, who were friendly to the American Colonies. He was privileged to meet the great British statesman, Edmund Burke, a great friend of the colonists in London, who spoke so eloquently in their behalf. When Stockton was questioned about America by one of the secretaries of state, he rejoiced that he had nothing to ask of the government "and therefore dare speak my sentiments without cringing. Whenever I can serve my native country, I leave no occasion untried." (Bill 27) He told them his strong feelings on the policy that had originated the Stamp Act, that was prudently repealed, and assured them that the colonies would never submit to be taxed by the British parliament without representation.

While in London he frequently attended Westminster Hall, and heard the arguments of Sir Fletcher Norton, John Dunning, Blackstone, and other celebrated sergeants and lawyers, who were distinguished by their eloquence and learning. He also was able to hear the opinions of such notables as Mansfield, Camden, Yates and other great men, who, at that period of British history, dignified the judicial character of the kingdom. He attended some of the theatrical performances and especially enjoyed Hamlet, particularly the ghost scene that "made his hair rise up" in his own words. He wrote Annis that he felt more cultivated and improved by his experiences in the theater and in London as a whole.

Following the fashion of the day, Annis gave herself and Richard the literary names of Emelia and Lucius, and it was thus that they signed their letters to each other. When the stories of his social successes in London reached Philadelphia, and Annis, who had been visiting, was teased about it, she wrote to him.

He replied:

> Had you received a letter I wrote you from Dublin and the one I wrote you upon my return here, you would have laughed at those idle people at Philadelphia who would persuade you that I would prefer the elegance of England to the sylvan shades of America. No, my dearest Emelia! The peaceful retreat which God has blessed me with at Princeton, you, and the sweet children you have brought me, are the sources from which I receive my highest earthly joys; joys which I prefer to the state of a prime minister or a king upon the throne. I am entertained with

the grandeur and variety of these kingdoms, as you wish me to be, and as you know I am curious, new objects are continually striking my attention and engaging my fancy; but one thought of thee puts all the pomp to flight; Priests, tapers, temples swim before my sight.

Again he wrote:

Let me tell you that all the grandeur and elegance that I have yet seen in these kingdoms, in different families where I have been received with great politeness, serves but to increase the pleasure I have for some years enjoyed in your society. I see not haughty imperious ignorant dame, but I rejoice that the partner of my life is so much her opposite. I see not a sensible, obliging, tender wife, but the image of my dear Emelia is full in view. Kiss my dear sweet children for me, and give rather the hardest squeeze to my only son, if you think it is right; if not, divide it equally without any partiality, but tell Dick I will bring him a laced hat, which seems to be his passion, and the little girls something pretty. Adieu, my dearest Emelia, may Heaven protect you and your dear little family until I meet you.

Annis was particularly pleased with any attention shown to her son Dick (John Richard), and Richard wrote: "Your friend, Lord Adam

Gordon, only returned from Scotland a few weeks ago. He was so obliging as to call immediately at my lodgings, and sent me an invitation to dine with him a few days after. He inquired very particularly after you and your dear little boy." (J.W. Stockton 1881)

Of the Queen's birth night ball he wrote: "Here I saw all your Duchesses of Ancaster, Hamilton, Etc., so famous for their beauty. But here I have done with this subject. For I had rather ramble with you along the rivulets of Morven and Red Hill and see the rural sports of the chaste little frogs, than again be at a birth night ball." (Bill 28)

Knowing of her love for their garden, Richard purchased plants and ornaments and even had drawings made for her of the lovely gardens of Britain. On his trip to Twickenham garden, Richard wrote to Annis from London in January 1767: "I shall take a gentleman who draws well, to lay down an exact plan of the whole. In this I shall take great pleasure, because I know how it will please you." Richard wanted to make Morven an estate with gardens that rivaled those of England. Annis was fond of their lovely garden and it held special feelings for her as she had spent many treasured hours in the garden with Richard, and when he died, she watched his carriage-hearse pass by from their garden.

He brought her a small piece of brick he found at Dover Castle, which he was told was built before the birth of Christ. He also brought her such treasures as a small piece of wood cut from an effigy of Archbishop Peckham, buried in Canterbury more than five hundred years before, and his most prized treasure..... a piece from the king's coronation chair.

The months of February and March, 1767, Richard spent in Scotland.

He was received with friendship and respect by many eminent noblemen, gentlemen, and literati, of that part of the kingdom. He spoke fondly of the manner, hospitality and politeness of the Earl of Leven. Later in America his family would return the kindness. This illustrious nobleman was the commander-in-chief of Edinburgh castle, and resided in the city. The Earl's hospitality towards respectable Americans was widely known, and he favored Richard Stockton with his friendship and soon afterward he was complimented with a public dinner where the Lord Provost and council of the city welcomed him officially. They conferred on him the freedom of the city, a testimony to his character and talents. This honor was acknowledged by Richard in an address delivered with the superior eloquence which distinguished him. (Sanderson 3: 86)

At this time he visited the ancient town of Paisley, to visit Rev. Doctor John Witherspoon, who had been recently elected president of the College of New Jersey. Witherspoon had declined the appointment because of the reluctance of his wife and daughters to immigrate to America. Richard was directed by the trustees of the college to employ all his powers of persuasion to reverse that decision. Happily, he was able to remove the objections with the aid of young Benjamin Rush, a friend of Richard Stockton and then a medical student in Edinburgh. Doctor Witherspoon accepted the nomination a short time later. Doctor Witherspoon was not only a material benefit to the college but to the country at large. His profound learning and distinguished character imparted celebrity to the college over which he presided, and the colonies found a powerful supporter during the Revolutionary War. Rev. Doctor John Witherspoon, like his friend Richard Stockton, became a signer of the Declaration of Independence, and young Benjamin Rush would become Dr. Benjamin Rush and marry Richard's daughter Julia. Dr. Benjamin Rush would also become a signer of the Declaration of Independence.

As he continued his tour through Great Britain, Richard arrived in Dublin in the month of October, 1766, where he was again received in a manner becoming his rank in society. During his short stay in Ireland, he noticed the contrast in conditions between the luxury of the wealthy and the miserable conditions of the poorer classes of society under the oppressions of the British government. He sympathized with the distressed people of Ireland and felt that the plan of the British ministry was to reduce his fellow countrymen to the same poverty at some point. (Sanderson 3: 88)

It is interesting to reveal two incidents that occurred during his residence in Great Britain, by which his life was placed in peril, and his country was almost deprived of one of its founding fathers and most eloquent advocates. He was attacked at night in the city of Edinburgh by a desperate robber. He defended himself skillfully with a small sword, and repelled the attack without serious injury; but the robber, although wounded made his escape. The robber hadn't realized that the well dressed gentleman he attacked was one of the finest swordsmen in the colonies.

The second time his life was preserved made an indelible impression on his mind, and he frequently related the circumstance and divine intervention which had saved him from destruction. He had booked passage on a ship to cross the Irish channel, but his baggage, did not arrive in time to make the trip. He was disappointed, but it proved to be his preservation. The ship he had booked sunk in a violent storm, and all aboard perished, including the British General Stanwise. He booked passage on another ship a few days later and passed the Irish channel in safety.

One of the most moving experiences of his trip was the opportunity to meet and spend time with the Earl of Chesterfield, distinguished as a politician, but still more as a man whose polished and fascinating manners made him the most distinguished gentleman of the era. Richard often talked with great pleasure of his interesting meeting with that nobleman. When first introduced to the Earl, his impression was that of an infirm old man, who had lost his teeth and his hearing, and was not very pleasing to look at. But when the Earl began to speak, the old man's image changed; his eyes became brilliant and his whole manner was so persuasive and enchanting that in the words of Richard Stockton, later relating the experience, "I forgot that he was deaf and without teeth, and he appeared to me remarkably handsome." (Sanderson 3: 91)

Richard was concerned about the general ignorance prevalent in Great Britain in relation to the American character and people, which was observed among all classes of society. They thought the Americans less cultured and beneath them. The word "Americans" came from English writers who used the term negatively, as a way of referring to a population unworthy of equal status with full-blooded Englishmen of the British Empire. The word was uttered as an insult that designated an inferior or subordinate people. He used every opportunity at hand to enlighten them and elevate the American character to the degree of just consideration that he thought it deserved. Had Richard Stockton's views and patriotic feelings been supported, and the British shown an interest in American rights and opinions, the British could possibly have avoided the war that freed the colonies and deprived the British King of the fairest jewel in his crown.

Richard Stockton was at all times a sensible and dignified speaker, remarkable for his determination and energy. He was a profound and scholarly lawyer, and his decisions and opinions while on the bench, in committees of congress, on admiralty questions and in the High Court of Errors of New Jersey was considered of high authority. His study of the great orators of antiquity, with whose writings, in the original languages, he was familiar, his acquaintance with the best writers of modern times and his practical opportunities of hearing the Ciceros and Demosthenes of Great Britain, uniting with his native genius, invested him with a superior and powerful eloquence, which has rarely been exceeded in this country. He also possessed a natural inclination towards music, and a refined taste for poetry, painting, and the fine arts in general. (Sanderson 3: 105)

BACK TO THE COLONIES

After an absence of 15 months Richard felt he had done his best to enlighten the British King, Parliament and the prominent men of Great Britain on the concerns of the colonies. He had happily persuaded Rev. Doctor John Witherspoon to immigrate with his family to the colonies and become the President of the College of New Jersey with the help of his friend young Benjamin Rush. He had made many friends but was homesick for his family and Country. In August, 1767 he boarded a vessel bound for New York. After twenty-six days he stepped off the ship and touched the soil of his beloved country. In New York he was met by his neighbors, relatives, and friends, who escorted him to his residence in Princeton, with the highest respect and affection.

It had been a long and lonely time for Annis and the children. It had also been a time of sadness for Annis as her mother had died while Richard was traveling. Her day was spent with the care of the children, and she was fortunate to have servants and Richard's brothers nearby, to help her care for Morven, the land and livestock. Richard was well known for the beautiful horses that he raised and took great pride in his livestock, crops and their lovely home, Morven. It had been a great endeavor for Annis, and she was happy to have her beloved husband back home at last.

In 1768 Richard was elevated to a seat in the royal legislative judiciary, and executive council of the province. In 1774 he, who had always dressed with quiet elegance, donned the splendid robes of a judge of the provincial Supreme Court. At that time he was high in the royal favor. He possessed an ample fortune, was surrounded by a family whom he greatly loved, and held a high and honorable station under the King of Great Britain. He was a good friend of royal governor William Franklin, the illegitimate son of Benjamin Franklin. He felt, after meeting King George III, that he was a good king who unfortunately had many advisors that held the colonies in low esteem. On his trip to England to meet with the king, Richard had met many important members of Parliament and had hoped to change their opinions of the people of the colonies. He felt that he succeeded with those he encountered, but was not able to meet all the members and some had their minds closed early on because he was an "American" and beneath them.

Richard and Annis enjoyed the pleasures of a high and respected position in government, and they were held in high regard by their friends and countrymen. Richard was known as a fair and honorable judge. He had shown time and again that he would be fair to the common man as well as the elite. When unadorned by the elaborate robes of judicial office that prevailed previous to the revolution, he was neat but simple in his dress. Before the Revolutionary War, the Stocktons lived in a state of splendor, frequently adopted by all distinguished men under the royal government, which the advantages of a country residence and the possession of affluence afforded them. Every stranger who visited his mansion was cordially welcomed in the genuine style of ancient hospitality, and it was customary in those days for travelers and visitors to call upon men of rank. Richard Stockton was the first Master of the

ELIAS BOUDINOT
Brother of Annis Stockton and married to Richard's sister, Hannah.
Portrait by Charles Willson Peale c. 1782
Courtesy Independence National Historical Park Collection

first chartered Masonic lodge (St. John's No. 1) in New Jersey. This was an extremely high honor. St. John's was chartered in Princeton on December 27, 1765. Richard visited with his Masonic brethren while in England and Scotland in 1766-67. Richard no doubt visited Rosslyn Chapel completed in 1486 near Edinburgh on his visit to the city, as it was a place of pilgrimage to Freemason's world wide. Benjamin Franklin likely introduced Masonry to Richard Stockton after Franklin made his

had to make
assumptions?

own trip to Edinburgh in 1759. Franklin was the Grand Master of the Philadelphia Lodge in 1735, and was later admitted to the highly select Nine Sisters Lodge in Paris. After viewing Rosslyn Chapel, Stockton and Franklin learned that the Earl of Orkney, Prince Henry Sinclair, grandfather of the chapel's donor had sailed to Massachusetts by way of Greenland in 1398. While there, they left a medieval knight chiseled out of rock at Westford, Massachusetts representing Sir James Gunn of Clyth, a companion of Sir Henry on his voyage to America. While in England he received his Stockton coat of arms with the motto "Omnia Deo Pendent," – all depends on God. Richard loved to ride his magnificent horses, and he practiced his swordsmanship with great pride, but his greatest pride was his family, Annis and his six young children whom he dearly loved. (Black 16)

While Richard was traveling overseas in 1766-67, his brother-in-law, Elias Boudinot, had taken charge of his law practice. Not only was Elias his wife's brother, he was also married to Richard's sister, Hanna. Elias studied law under the supervision of Richard Stockton, became a lawyer, and went on to become a member of the committee of safety in 1775. He was appointed by General George Washington to be commissary general of prisoners in the Revolutionary Army 1776-1779. He was a member of the Continental Congress in 1778, 1781-1783. He served as President of Congress in 1782 and 1783, and signed the treaty of peace with England. He was elected to the First, Second, and Third Congresses (March 4, 1789-March 3, 1795); and became Director of the Mint from October 1795 to July 1805. He was elected first president of the

American Bible Society, in 1816. He served for 49 years as a trustee of the College of New Jersey (Princeton University). Elias Boudinot died in Burlington, New Jersey, October 24, 1821 and is buried in St. Mary's Protestant Episcopal Church Cemetery.

Elias Boudinot is responsible for our Thanksgiving Holiday, for it was Elias that proposed on September 25, 1789, in the United States House of Representatives a resolution that we officially celebrate a day of public thanksgiving. After much debate, it was finally agreed on, and President Washington issued a proclamation designating a day of prayer and thanksgiving. Elias Boudinot was a favorite brother of Annis, and she wrote to him frequently. Elias took young John Richard under his supervision to educate after the death of Richard Stockton. John Richard became known as Richard after his father's death and was also affectionately called the "Duke" and became an eminent lawyer, a congressman and a Senator from New Jersey.

In 1772, a red-headed young man of 15 appeared on the doorstep of Elias Boudinot. The young man had a letter of introduction from a minister in St. Croix, West Indies. His name was Alexander Hamilton, and he lived with the Boudinot family for two years. In the summer of 1774, while Elias and Hanna enjoyed the company of the young Alexander, their sweet young baby daughter Maria, fell ill. To enable the worried father and distraught mother to gain some rest, Alexander sat up with the child. All efforts to save her were in vain and unfortunately she died. Thinking to comfort the bereaved parents, the future co-author of the Federalist Papers composed a set of verses:

For the sweet babe; my doating heart
Did all a Mother's fondness feel;
Carefull to act each tender part
And guard from evry threatening ill.

But what, alas! Availd my care?
The unrelenting hand of death,
Regardless of a parent's prayr,
Has stopped my lovely Infant's breath.

Thou'rt gone, forever gone—yet where?
Ah! pleasing thought; to endless bliss.
Then, why Indulge the rising tear?
Canst thou, fond heart, lament for this?

Let reason silence nature's strife,
And weep Maria's fate no more;
She's safe from all the storms of life,
And wafted to a peaceful Shore.

It is interesting that the Stocktons and Boudinots were both closely associated with Alexander Hamilton and Aaron Burr. Aaron's parents were Annis Stockton's closest friends before they died of smallpox in 1758. Of course, in later years Vice President Aaron Burr would kill Alexander Hamilton in a duel.

Alexander wrote poem for death of baby

CLOUDS OF REBELLION

Richard Stockton had struggled at first toward reconciliation between the colonies and Britain and on December 12, 1774; he drew up and sent to Lord Dartmouth, Secretary for the Colonies, "An Expedient for the Settlement of the American Disputes," which was a plan for the self-government of America, independent of Parliament but still owing allegiance to the English Crown. If something of the kind were not done, he warned the noble lord, the result would be an obstinate, awful, and tremendous war. He held out for peaceful measures long after other members of his family had changed their views to support independence.

His brother-in-law Elias Boudinot was counsel for the defense in an action brought by the East India Tea Company for destruction of tea in New Jersey. When Elias' daughter Susan, only nine years old, was served a cup of tea at the home of the royal governor Franklin (tea being a source of irritation to the colonists and no longer used in many homes in protest of the tea tax), she curtsied, raised the cup to her lips, and tossed the contents of her teacup out an open window, to the amusement of her parents, and probably one of America's first female protesters. Richard and Annis also in attendance, no doubt also thought it amusing.

Can We Gain Independency?

A Continent of 1000 miles Sea Coast defending themselves with-out one Ship of War against 300 Battle

Ships completely manned and fitted…A Country that can pay but 30 thousand men, at War with a Nation that had paid, and can pay 150 Thousand…a Country of three millions of inhabitants, fighting with a Nation of 15 million…A Country that can raise but 1 Mil. Of Money at War with a Nation who can raise 20 Mil. In specie…A Country without Arms, without Ammunition, without Trade, contending with a Nation that enjoys the whole in the fullest Latitude." (*New Hampshire Gazette*, January 1776)

These questions were certainly on the minds of Richard and many other patriots in 1776 as the talk of Independence from England was discussed.

Annis struggled with the moderate feelings of her husband and her more revolutionary brother Elias. Possibly, Richard's father's upbringing as a Quaker and his Quaker ancestors' feelings of non-violence had made him eager to have the British understand his feelings about self rule, or at least for the colonies to be given representation in Parliament and avoid a bloody war.

When at last all his attempts to change the minds of the British failed, he decided he must, when given a choice of King or country, choose his country. He resigned his royal appointments and made a public disavowal of his support of Britain. He was shortly thereafter made a member of the Continental Congress.

"On June 15, the provincial legislature of New Jersey had ordered the arrest of its royal governor, William Franklin, the estranged, illegitimate son of Benjamin Franklin, and authorized its delegates in Congress to vote for independence. To see that this was done, five new New Jersey delegates including Stockton had been appointed." (McCullough 122)

DRAFTING THE DECLARATION OF INDEPENDENCE
THE COMMITTEE - FRANKLIN, JEFFERSON, ADAMS, LIVINGSTON, SHERMAN
Engraved from the original painting by Chappel, Johnson, Fray, and Co. Publishers, New York, 1870
From the authors' private collection

On June 11th, a committee of five was chosen to prepare a declaration. Those members were Thomas Jefferson, John Adams, Benjamin Franklin, Roger Sherman, and Phillip Livingston. Two days later the committee members met but Benjamin Franklin was not present for the meetings, as he was suffering from an attack of the gout. Jefferson was given the task of writing the document. Jefferson had suggested Adams, who had worked the hardest and longest for independence should write the Declaration. Adams declined and when questioned by Jefferson as to his reasons for declining Adams remarked "Reason first - You are a Virginian, and a Virginian ought to appear at the head of this business. Reason second - I am obnoxious, suspected, and unpopular. You are very much otherwise. Reason third - You can write ten times better than I can." (Hawke 129)

On July 1, 1776 Richard Stockton and his good friend Rev. John Witherspoon arrived in Philadelphia to take their place as new members of Congress meeting at the State House (now Independence Hall). It had been a long and muddy ride from Princeton, they had been caught in a violent thunderstorm, and their clothes were soaking wet. Because of the storm they had arrived late, at the end of a speech John Adams was giving in favor of independence. As they had not been present for the entire speech Richard asked Adams to repeat what they had missed. Adams at first refused, but when Stockton again repeated his request, and at the urging of Edward Rutledge who said "only Adams had the facts at his command", Adams rose to the occasion and gave a rousing speech in favor of independence. Richard was silent during Adams' speech and then listened with thoughtful and respectful attention to the arguments that were offered by supporters and opponents of the declaration under consideration. After hearing the irresistible and conclusive arguments of the honorable John Adams for independence, Richard fully concurred in the final vote in favor of that bold and decisive measure. Richard gave a short but energetic speech at the close of the debate. Richard declared Adams "the Atlas of the hour, the man to whom the country is most indebted for the great measure of independency. He who sustained the debate, and by the force of reasoning demonstrated not only the justice, but the expediency of the measure." (McCullough 127)

During the long debate Joseph Hewes of North Carolina, who earlier had opposed separation from Britain, "started suddenly upright, and lifting up both his hands to Heaven, as if he had been in a trance, cried out, 'It is done! And I will abide by it.'" (128) The debate lasted until nearly seven in the evening, but when a preliminary vote was taken four colonies held back and refused to proclaim independence. New York abstained, saying they lacked instructions. Pennsylvania voted no, as did South Carolina. Delaware was divided, and Delaware delegate Caesar Rodney, who was in favor of independence, was sent for.

Richard Stockton and several delegates met at the City Tavern that night and learned that over one hundred British ships had been sighted off New York, according to John Covenhoven of New Jersey. That number eventually grew to over four hundred. The delegates were certainly alarmed, but by the end of the next day, July 2, all but New York voted for independence. Just before Congress adjourned for the evening, Caesar Rodney of Delaware had appeared covered with mud from head to toe and still "booted and spurred." (129) Tall and thin, he wore a green silk scarf to cover the skin cancer on the side of his face. He had ridden eighty miles through a storm, changing horses several times, to cast his vote for independence. John Dickinson and Robert Morris, both against independence at that time, had absented themselves from the meeting, and the remaining Pennsylvania delegation then voted in favor of independence. Morris later signed the Declaration but Dickinson never did.

> John Adams wrote to his wife Abigail: The second day of July 1776 will be the most memorable epocha in the history of America. I am apt to believe that it will be celebrated by succeeding generations as the great anniversary festival. It ought to be commemorated as the Day of Deliverance by solemn acts of devotion to God Almighty. It ought to be solemnized with pomp and parade, with shows, games, sports, guns, bells, bonfires, and illuminations from one end of this country to the other from this time forward forever more. (McCullough 130)

Since New York had not voted in favor of independence, the broadside copy prepared on July 4, 1776, and signed by only John

Hancock and Secretary Thompson said "A Declaration by the Representatives of the United States of America in General Congress Assembled." After New York agreed to independence on July 15, the Declaration read "The Unanimous Declaration of the thirteen United States of America." It was the job of Timothy Matlack to engross the Declaration of Independence on parchment so all delegates could later sign it.

Richard stayed with Julia and Benjamin Rush while he attended Congress, and enjoyed their company. The meetings of Congress lasted until nearly nine in the evening. During the hot summer months it was more comfortable in the evenings. The doors of Congress were kept closed and locked and the windows were closed, so quarrelling voices would not be heard on the street outside. The room that the delegates met in was large, and made to seem larger by the luminous white walls. The room was nicely furnished with tables and comfortable wooden chairs. On the back wall, facing the President's desk was a panoply – that consisted of a drum, swords, and banners seized from Fort Ticonderoga the previous year. Ethan Allen and Benedict Arnold had captured the Fort, shouting that they were taking it "in the name of the Great Jehovah and the Continental Congress!" (Limbaugh 1) Ethan Allen was later captured and imprisoned in Provost Prison and then paroled by General Howe in New York. Benedict Arnold would become a traitor to his country. Richard Stockton would visit Fort Ticonderoga a few months later at the request of Congress. The day was spent attempting to keep the voracious horseflies that somehow found their

THE ANNOUNCEMENT OF THE DECLARATION OF INDEPENDENCE STATE HOUSE, PHILADELPHIA

Engraved by J. McGoffin at J. M. Butler's establishment
from the authors' private collection

way into the room, from biting necks and legs right through silk stockings. It was reported that all discussion was punctuated by the slap of hands on necks and legs. Many a night Richard and Benjamin stopped by the City Tavern to meet with other delegates and discuss events of Congress on their way home.

On July 8, outside the Pennsylvania State House, the Declaration of Independence was first read to the public. After it was read, people cheered, bells rang out and soldiers paraded.

On July 9, 1776, the Declaration of Independence was proclaimed at Princeton. "Last night Nassau Hall was grandly illuminated, and Independency proclaimed under a triple volley of musketry, and universal acclamation for the prosperity of the United States. The ceremony was conducted with the greatest decorum."(American Archives).

In New York, the Declaration was read aloud to Washington's assembled troops. That night a crowd pulled down the equestrian statue of George III, and it was reportedly melted down to make ammunition. The large noisy crowd then celebrated with bonfires, and toasts everywhere across town.

On August 2, 1776, Richard Stockton was the eleventh signer of fifty to affix his signature to the Declaration of Independence, and over the next five years, six other signers added their signatures. The last signer was Thomas McKean signing in 1781.

Anecdotes abound on the signing of the engrossed copy on August 2, 1776. Hancock supposedly remarked: "There! John Bull can read my name without his spectacles." Stephen Hopkins, afflicted with the palsy, remarked: "My hand trembles, but my heart does not!" Benjamin Franklin supposedly said: "We must all hang together, or most assuredly we shall all hang separately." Benjamin Rush wrote that Benjamin Harrison, a rather heavy man looked over at William Ellery's thin frame and said, "I shall have a great advantage over you, Mr. Ellery, when we are all hung for what we are now doing. From the size and weight of my body I shall die in a few minutes, but from the lightness of your body you will dance in the air an hour or two before you are dead." (Hawke 194) Rush recalled, "this speech procured a transient smile, but it was soon succeeded by the solemnity with which the whole business was conducted." (Hawke 194)

The remarks made by Hancock and Hopkins may be true, but the following accounts of the day are corroborated by Benjamin Rush as he recalled the day, and the signing of the Declaration of Independence in a letter to John Adams in 1811. Rush wrote "The pensive and awful silence which pervaded the house when we were called up, one after another, to the table of the President of Congress to subscribe what was believed by many at that time to be our own death warrants." (Hawke 194) Such was the courage and dedication to this country by Richard Stockton and the other signers.

Richard showed his accustomed diligence and ability
in the performance of his congressional duties, and was
frequently appointed to the more important committees.

His acute perceptions, logical powers of reasoning, superior eloquence, and matured experience of men and things, united with a profound knowledge of law and politics, were appreciated by his associates, among whom he held a distinguished rank. (Sanderson 2: 192)

Back home to visit his family in late August, Richard attended a meeting in Princeton. On August 27, 1776 at the first joint meeting of the state delegates under the new constitution, William Livingston and Richard Stockton were the first republican candidates for the office of governor. On the first ballot they received an equal number of votes. The second ballot gave Livingston the office of governor by one vote. Richard was immediately chosen, by unanimous vote, to be chief justice of the state, but he declined, preferring to keep his seat in the Continental Congress.

Richard returned to Philadelphia and during the autumn of 1776, he continued to tend to his duties in Congress. On September 26, he and George Clymer of Pennsylvania were sent on their arduous journey of nearly two month's duration to inspect the northern army. They were empowered by Congress to contract for provisions; provide barracks and clothing for the troops; make regulation for the hospitals; assist in the military councils as the best mode of re-enlisting the army; and finally, to report to Congress on the state of the army, and any regulations they might think necessary for its better supply. They had traveled to Albany, Saratoga, Ticonderoga, and every facility necessary to implement their mission, aided by General Schuyler, who commanded the northern army. They had found the army in need of all necessary things such as provisions, medical care, weapons, warm clothing, shoes and stockings. There was no place to acquire these items and unfortunately no money to purchase them with, if they were to be found. They had to depend on Congress and the states to provide for the army and help for the army was slow in coming, if it came at all.

Richard had written to Abraham Clark of New Jersey a fellow member of Congress on October 28, 1776:

> Dear Sir, Before I left Philadelphia Congress appointed a Committee, consisting of one member from each state, to devise ways and means for furnishing the Army with clothing and etc. As the member appointed for New Jersey, I laid the resolution before our Legislature then sitting at Princeton, and recommended to them the great importance of their approaching persons in every county. They were pleased to take up the matter with that zeal which the nature of it required and determined to take every step that they might in this endeavor to more effectually and speedily execute the business. I hope therefore that already a considerable quantity of shoes and stockings at least may be provided and that you will take immediate order for the sending of the parcels. Col. Dayton's Regiment is moved from Fort Stanwix to Tyconderoga the Col. and Major

Barber came here last evening and the Regiment is now within a few miles of this place, marching with cheerfulness, but a great part of the men barefooted and barelegged. My heart melts with compassion for my brave countrymen who are thus venturing their lives in the public service and yet so distressed. There is not a single shoe or stocking to be had in this part of the world, or I would ride a hundred miles through the woods, and purchase them with my own money—for you'll consider that the weather here must be different from that in New Jersey; it is very cold now I assure you. For God's sake my dear sir, upon the receipt of this collect all the shoes and stocking you can, and send them off for Albany in light wagons; a couple of two horse wagons will bring a great many, which may be distributed among our several Regiments who will be all together at Tyconderoga in a few days—If any Breeches, gloves and coats be ready send them along; but do not wait for them if the shoes and stockings are ready, and the others not—we have dispatches from General Gates this morning informing that he hourly expects to be attacked by the Enemy; but our works are very strong and a Boom thrown across the water from Tyconderoga to prevent the enemies shipping from getting below us, therefore I trust, with the blessing of Almighty God, that we shall disappoint their wishes and sanguinary purposes—But shall the brave troops from New Jersey stand in lines half leg deep in snow without shoes or stocking—God forbid. I shall empty my portmanteau of the stockings I have for my own use on this journey, excepting a pair to take back home, but this is a drop of water in the Ocean." (Letter of Richard Stockton to Abraham Clark, Historical Society of Princeton, N.J.)

His heartfelt compassion for his fellow countrymen in such dire need of every thing from shoes, clothing, guns, food and blankets was apparent. Such was the character of this great patriot. He would ride a hundred miles through the woods to buy shoes and stockings for his men with his own money, and a month later he would be made to walk 20 miles in only stockings through the mud and freezing weather to jail in Perth Amboy by his loyalist captors.

In 1775 their oldest daughter Julia had become a lovely young lady, and young men of the College of New Jersey vied for her attention. She had long dark hair and a beautiful face that favored her father's good looks. Like her mother, Julia could read, write and play a musical instrument. There was a young bachelor that came to visit his friend Richard Stockton in the summer of 1775. His name was Dr. Benjamin Rush, he was 30 years old, born near Philadelphia, and he had assisted Richard Stockton in convincing Reverend Dr. John Witherspoon to take the position of President of the college of New Jersey while a student of medicine at the University of Edinburgh in Scotland in 1767. He had graduated from the College of New Jersey at Princeton when only 14 years of age.

Dear Sir,

Before I left Philada. Congress appointed a committee, consisting of one member from each State, to devise ways & means for furnishing the Army with Clothing &c. As the member appointed for New Jersey, I laid the resolution before our Legislature then sitting at Princeton, and recommended to them the great importance of their appointing persons in every county — they were pleased to take up the matter with that zeal which the nature of it required and determined to take a sweep, that they might, in their answers, the more effectually & speedily execute the business. I hope therefore that already a considerable quantity of Shoes & Stockings, at least may be provided, and that you will take immediate order for the sending a part of it ~~~~~~~~~~~~~~~~~~~~~~~~~

Col. Dayton's Regiment is arrived from Fort Stanwix & is on the way — the Col. and Major Barber came here last evening and the Regiment is now within a few miles of this place, marching with cheerfulness, but great part of the men barefoot & bare legged.

My heart melts with compassion for my brave countrymen who are thus venturing their lives in the public service, and yet are so distressed. There is not a single Shoe or Stocking to be had in this part of the world, ~~though side a hundred miles thro' the woods~~ and purchase them with my own money — for you'll consider that the weather there must be very different from that in N. Jersey; it is very cold now I assure you. For God's sake, my dear Sir, upon the rect. of this collect all the Shoes & Stockings you can, and send them ff for Albany in light Waggons; a couple of two horse Waggons will bring a great many, which may be distributed among our several Regiments also will be all together at Ticonderoga in a few days — if any Breeches greatcoats be ready send them along; but do not wait for them, if the Shoes & Stockings are ready, and the others not — we have dispatches from Genl Gates this morning informing that he hourly expects to be attacked by the Enemy; but our works he doing strong, and to Boom thereon they be water from Lyon drove to Mount Independence to prevent the enemies' shipping from getting below us, therefore I trust, with the blessing of almighty God, that we shall disappoint their wicked & sanguinary purposes — But shall the brave troops from New Jersey stand in the lines half leg deep in Snow without Shoes or Stockings — God forbid. I shall empty my portmanteau of the Stockings I have for my own use on this journey, excepting a pair to take and have — but this is a drop of water in the Ocean — In the

Your most obedt humble servt

Rich'd Stockton

Mr Stockton's Letter to Abraham Clark Esq 28 Oct'r 1776

Al. Clark Esqr.

Historical Society of Princeton
Letter by Richard Stockton (signer)
to Abraham Clark, 1776

115

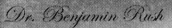

Dr. Benjamin Rush
Portrait by Charles Willson Peale, 1776
Courtesy, Winterthur Museum
Gift of Mrs. Julie B. Henry

Mrs. Julia Stockton Rush
Portrait by Charles Willson Peale, 1783
Courtesy, Winterthur Museum
Gift of Mrs. Julie B. Henry

Benjamin Rush was a handsome, well-spoken gentleman. After spending a few days with the Stocktons, he was quite taken with young Julia. She could speak well on most subjects and was remarkably well read for one so young. Benjamin was infatuated with the intelligent and beautiful daughter of his good friend, and they were soon engaged to be married. Benjamin Rush had opened a medical practice in Philadelphia in 1769 and was appointed a Professor of Chemistry at the College of Philadelphia at that time. He was beloved in his city, where he practiced extensively among the poor. He published the first American textbook on Chemistry. In 1773 he contributed editorial essays to the papers about the patriot cause. He was active in the Sons of Liberty in Philadelphia during that time and had recommended the title "Common Sense" to his friend Thomas Paine for a pamphlet he was writing that would become extremely popular among patriots.

Rush wrote an essay on slavery that brought him into public affairs. He wrote, "Remember, the eyes of all Europe are fixed upon you to preserve an asylum for freedom in this country, after the last pillars of it are fallen in every other quarter of the globe." Slavery is a crime against God and man, and "national crimes require national punishments," he warned. He further wrote "Remember, my countrymen, the present era - perhaps the present struggle - will fix the constitution of America forever. Think of your ancestors and of your posterity." (Hawke 70)

On one visit to the Stocktons when Julia was a child of four, it was Benjamin Rush that carried her home when she fell asleep at a college commencement. Now he would carry her over the threshold as his

17-year-old bride.

On January 11, 1776, Benjamin married the lovely Julia Stockton. The Reverend Dr. John Witherspoon officiated, and a reception was held at the Stockton home "Morven". In June 1776, Rush was elected to attend the provincial conference to send delegates to the Continental Congress. He was appointed to represent Pennsylvania that year and so signed the Declaration of Independence. In April 1777 he was appointed Surgeon General of the department of the Continental Army and in July 1777 he was made Physician General. He was with the army at the battles of Trenton and Princeton and cared for the wounded. He was critical of the administration of the Army Medical service under Dr. William Shippen, and felt the conditions were deplorable and complained to Washington, who deferred to the Congress. Ultimately Congress upheld Shippen, and Rush resigned in disgust.

Benjamin Rush was with General Washington on December 24, 1776 when Rush wrote:

> I spent a night at a farm house near to him, and the next morning passed near an hour with him in private. He appeared much depressed, and lamented the ragged and dissolving state of his army in affecting terms. I gave him assurance of the disposition of Congress to support him, under his present difficulties and distresses. While I was talking to him, I observed him to play with his pen and ink upon several small pieces of paper. One of them by

accident fell upon the floor near my feet. I was struck with the inscription upon it. It was "Victory or Death". Rush goes on to say, On the following evening I was ordered by General Cadwallider to attend the militia at Dunk's ferry. An attempt was made to cross the Delaware at that place by Gen. Cadwallider in order to cooperate with General Washington the next morning in an attack upon the river. Great bodies of floating ice rendered the passage of the river impracticable. We returned to Bristol in a heavy snow storm in the middle of the night. The next morning we heard that General Washington had been more successful in crossing the river above Trenton, and that he had surprised and taken 1000 Hessians at that place. General Cadwallider followed him to the Jersey shore on the afternoon of the same day, and we slept at Burlington with his detachment the next night. The next day we marched to Bordentown and from thence to Crosswicks where we remained for two days. I had reason to believe here, that in my interview with General Washington, he had been meditating upon his attack upon the Hessians at their posts on the Jersey side of the Delaware; for I found that the countersign of his troops at the surprise of Trenton was "Victory or Death". (Corner 124)

When Dr. Benjamin Rush learned of the capture and brutal prison treatment his father-in-law Richard Stockton had received at the hands of the Loyalists (Tory) and British, he was incensed. He wrote to Richard Henry Lee: "Every particle of my blood is electrified with revenge, and if justice cannot be done him in any other way, I declare I will, in defiance of the authority of the Congress and the power of the army, drive the first rascally Tory I meet a hundred miles, barefooted, through the first deep snow that falls in our country." (Hess 398)

Dr. Benjamin Rush was the only signer to travel with the Continental Army as a Doctor. Richard Stockton and George Clymer traveled with the army at the request of Congress. Rush experienced first hand the real war while engaged in battle and treating the horrible wounds inflicted on the soldiers. George Walton, Thomas Heyward, and Edward Rutledge fought with their local militias as did other signers.

Another twist of fate would be that when Benjamin Rush was a student at the University of Edinburgh, he was a friend of the Earl of Leven and was acquainted with his children. Richard Stockton on his journey to Scotland was entertained by The Earl at Edinburgh Castle. In 1781, Edinburgh Castle was used by the British to incarcerate American prisoners of war in dungeons. The wooden doors and stone walls reveal the markings made by the American prisoners. During the battle of Princeton, the Earl's young son, Captain the Hon. William Leslie of the British army and nephew of Brigadier-General Alexander Leslie, was severely wounded, and in his pocket a letter was found from Dr. Benjamin Rush to William Leslie saying "should the fortune of war throw him into the hands of the American army, to show the letter to

General Washington or General Lee, either of whom would, I expect, indulge him in a parole to visit Philadelphia, where I begged he would make my house his home." Rush learned of Captain Leslie's death from another wounded British officer. When Dr. Rush went to attend Capt. McPherson's wound he was introduced. Captain McPherson exclaimed, "Are you Dr. Rush, Captain Leslie's friend?" Rush said he was, and McPherson said "Oh! Sir, he loved you like a brother." (Corner 129) Rush had Captain Leslie buried with the honors of war, in the church yard at Pluckamin, New Jersey. In the summer of 1777 Benjamin Rush visited Capt. Leslie's grave and plucked a blade of grass from it, and placed a stone marker over it with an inscription designating his age, family, rank in the army and the time and manner of his death. Rush wrote to William Leslie's sister Lady Jane Belsches (Stuart) about this in a letter a few years later. In her answer to this letter she said "Why did you not send me that blade of grass? I would have preserved it forever with my tears." (Corner 129) The Earl told of this act of kindness was overcome with emotion to know that Rush had provided a marker and been with his son an ocean apart.

CAPTAIN LESLIE'S GRAVE INSCRIPTION

In Memory of the
Honble Captn Willm Leslie
of the 17th British Regiment
Son of the Earl of Leven
in Scotland

He fell Jany 3d 1777 Aged
26 Years at the battle of
Princeton
His friend Benjn Rush, M.D. of
Philadelphia
hath caused this Stone
to be erected as a mark
of his esteem for his WORTH
and of his respect
for his noble family

Resuming the practice of medicine, Rush helped found the Pennsylvania Hospital in Philadelphia, became president of the Philadelphia medical society, established the first free medical clinic for the poor in 1786, and continued to teach medicine at the University of Pennsylvania. He became world famous because of his dedication to duty during Philadelphia's two great yellow fever epidemics in 1793 and 1798 that killed approximately 8,000 persons. He discovered a cure for lockjaw and was honored for his contributions to medical science by medals and presents from the King of Prussia, the Queen of Italy, and the Czar of Russia.

In 1789, Benjamin Rush wrote in Philadelphia newspapers in favor of adopting the Federal constitution. He was then elected to the Pennsylvania convention which adopted that constitution. He was appointed treasurer of the US Mint where he served from 1797 to 1813.

His teaching and medical practice continued until the end of his life. He became the Professor of medical theory and clinical practice at the University of Pennsylvania in 1791, where he was a popular figure at the height of his influence in medicine and in social circles. He was a social activist, a prominent advocate for the abolition of slavery, and advocate for scientific education for the masses, including women, and for public clinics to treat the poor. He believed in providing treatment for the mentally ill, treating them with compassion and was known as the father of psychiatry. Rush was responsible for bringing John Adams and Thomas Jefferson back together after they drifted apart and was always a good friend and correspondent to both. When Dr. Benjamin Rush died in 1813, Thomas Jefferson wrote John Adams that "a better man than Rush could not have left us, more benevolent, more learned, of finer genius, or more honest," to which Adams replied he knew "of no Character living or dead, who has done more real good in America." To Rush's widow, Adams wrote, "There was no one outside his own family whose friendship was so essential to his happiness." (McCullough 612)

When Benjamin Rush died at the age of sixty-eight at his home in Philadelphia, he was the most celebrated physician in America. He and Julia had thirteen children and frequently visited Annis in Princeton. Julia Stockton Rush died at the age of eighty-nine on July 7, 1848 and is buried with her husband in Christ Church Cemetery in Philadelphia. Several signers of the Declaration of Independence are buried there including Benjamin Franklin.

THE FINAL STRUGGLE

important ch.

After his release from prison, and when his health would permit him, Richard attempted to earn a living by reopening his law practice and teaching new law students. He would never be the man he had been health-wise, and he struggled to make a living and support his family during this awful time of war. It would be nearly a year before his health was somewhat restored and he could travel any long distance, but it would take almost two years before he was nearly back to normal according to Dr. Benjamin Rush. In the small town of Princeton times were hard for everyone, not only the Stockton's. Richard and Annis were able to survive because of the generosity of her brother Elias, and friends that helped them in their time of need.

As President of the college, John Witherspoon was out of a job, as the College of New Jersey remained closed and was being used as a Continental army hospital. Witherspoon remained a member of Congress. The community was burdened by the demands of the Continental troops for firewood among other things, and the town was constantly threatened by the possibility of another British takeover. Governor Livingston and other members of the Legislature visited Richard frequently, and he was finally able to travel thirty miles to Philadelphia on legal business.

In 1777, Elizabeth Fergusson, a lifelong friend of his wife Annis, was in need of a good lawyer as she was about to lose her estate. She was a wealthy woman who had a few years before the war, married Henry

Hugh Fergusson. When the revolution began, he became a Tory. Elizabeth stood to lose all her property and belongings to the confiscation of Tory properties by the Pennsylvania government because of her marriage to Fergusson. Rumors had now been spread about her, and she was accused of passing messages to the British army and without the help of her good friends Richard and Annis Stockton, Elizabeth Fergusson would have lost all. Richard used his legal expertise to help her with the charges made against her. He had nothing to fear from his fellow citizens or New Jersey, and Pennsylvania authorities.

Nothing was written about doubts of Richard's loyalty in the papers of Congress or in any newspapers of the time. The letters he wrote show that he was under no suspicion at anytime. No member of Congress ever remarked that he was not trusted, nor was he ever spoken about in a disparaging way. Books of the time never mentioned any thing negative about Richard Stockton. His fellow members of Congress, and the citizens that knew him were mindful of the sacrifices he had made for his country, and treated him with the utmost respect and gratitude.

Richard and Annis struggled to rebuild Morven to its original condition. After Richard returned to his law practice and earned enough money, they slowly furnished their home again. Lord Cornwallis and his men had so abused their home that it took years to completely restore the house, the crops and livestock. As he struggled to recover his health and fortune, he was dealt another blow. He developed a lesion on his lip that would not heal.

On November 30, 1778, just two years after his capture by the British, he wrote to Annis from Philadelphia:

> I hoped to have finished at Gloucester last Saturday, but must return this week for a few days; after that I must pay all my attention to my poor lip, it is not worse I think than when I left you, but my mind is in a continued state of uneasiness about it—for your sake and that of the dear children, as well as my own, I trust God that I may be relieved. I have got your muff and tippet, and shall attend to your other memorandums, for all your requests within my power, have the effect of commands. Love to the children all—your most affectionate Richard Stockton.

When the next letter arrived Annis was left breathless as she read:

Philadelphia, Wed 9th Dec 1778

> My dear Love, I have carefully concealed from you the state of my lip for some time past, until by the blessing of God I could give you some agreeable tidings. I have now the pleasure to inform you that yesterday, at one o'clock; the malignant part was extracted by Dr. Jones, in the presence of several others of the faculty, whom I had consulted. You'll readily conceive the anxiety of mind I have possessed since I left you - for I upon my first coming

to this town, I found that it must be cut out. Dr. Jones concluded to attend me at home, at first; but I well knew the additional distress I should receive from the anxiety which would fill you and the children—I therefore very speedily concluded to have it done here, and in the meantime to prevent your distress by concealing it from you. I trust God that it is totally extracted, for they have made a large hole in my lip—they say it will grow up again. I thank God for the fortitude and patience he was pleased to grant me before and at the time of the operation. I did not utter a sigh, or move a muscle. I have also abundant reason to bless God for the ease and comfort I feel now—I have not the least pain, and a comfortable night, the last.—I was uneasy for about two hours after the operation, but the anodine [sic] they gave me immediately upon tying up the wound, composed me, and I feel as easy today, as I ever did in my life—as an evidence of it, I have come down from my chamber and am writing this in the parlour. I am thus particular as I know how greedily you will catch at everything that gives you any information respecting this interesting [illegible]. I cannot be certain of the day in which I shall return home; but it may be sometime next week—perhaps by the middle. In the midst of my own distresses I have been much concerned to hear, by Polly's letter that you have had the rheumatism: I hope it has been of short duration— My love to the Girls, and all the lesser children—poor little creatures! I know how much they will feel for me, among the rest. Julia [Mrs. Rush, at whose house he was staying] was remarkably preserved yesterday in a fall of the top of a Chest of drawers, while she was pulling out the bottom drawer—she [illegible] and fainted, but received no considerable hurt, as they went over her head—God be praised for his repeated mercies. Adieu my dearest, and be assured of my unremitting and constant affection.

Annis was on the next coach to Philadelphia to join her husband. When she arrived, the doctors were in disagreement, and Dr. Jones, considered the best surgeon in America, had prescribed a most meager diet and forbidden wine. Dr. Benjamin Rush disagreed saying such a total change of diet for a nearly fifty year old man would not be good for him and probably produce a "scrofulous tumor" in the neck that would be more dangerous than the lip had been. Dr. Jones won out and Richard followed the meager diet. They were hopeful that the operation was a success. Unfortunately that would not be the outcome. (Bill 49)

In April 1779, Richard wrote to his sister Hannah Boudinot that the cancer had spread to his throat, and he returned to Philadelphia for a second operation. It was too late, and throughout the next two years Richard was never free of pain unless under the influence of anodynes, and near the end of 1780 his agony had become such that Annis wrote a letter to her good friend Elizabeth Graeme Fergusson on November 24, 1780 stating Richard's condition.

If you could for a moment witness my situation, you would not wonder at my silence, totally confined to the chamber of a dear and dying husband, whose nerves have become so Irritable as not to be able, to bear the Scraping of a pen, on paper in his room, or Even the folding up of a letter, which deprives me of one of the greatest relief's I could have, in my present situation for alas I have leisure, painful leisure enough, thro all the tedious length of November nights, these nights, that in the zenith of their dark domain are Sunshine to the prospect of my mind, I use Doctor Young's words, because I can use none of my own, that can so well describe the feelings of my heart - for Indeed my dear friend, I am now all together discouraged, I have kept up my courage by constantly flattering myself, that the ulcer would heal, but it proves so obstinate that his constitution is sinking very fast under it, and I have been very apprehensive for a week past, that he could not survive long, but he is now a little better - he desired me when I wrote, to give his most affectionate regards to you, and tell you that he never should see you more, in the world, but that he should die as he had lived, for a great many years, your tender and sympathizing friend-pardon me my dear, I can write no more on this subject, and must conclude with telling you, that your last letter, as well as all others, are a cordial to me and therefore I doubt not, but you will remember, me, in the midst of my own distress I am not unmindful of yours, and sympathize most sincerely with you, my affectionate wishes to my dear friend Miss Stedman, and believe me hers and yours in the Bonds of Amity. A. Stockton

Annis wrote a poem about Richard and her grief:

> While through the silence of the gloomy night
> My aching heart reverb'rates every groan,
> And watching by the glimmering taper's light,
> I make each sigh, each mortal pang my own.
>
> Oh! Could I take the fate to him assigned,
> And leave the helpless family their head!
> How pleased, how peaceful to my lot resigned,
> I'd quit the nurses's station for the bed.

In February 1780, a young Robert Troup proposed to young Aaron Burr, newly resigned from the Continental army, that they should study the law under Richard Stockton, unfortunately Richard's health would not permit that to occur. The exposure to disease and the inhuman treatment he received while a prisoner in New York possibly laid the foundation for the disease from which he could not recover.

Annis, who had shared his brighter fortunes, now cheered him in his declining days with her tenderness and devotion. She nursed him through his long and painful illness, and she along with the children, attempted to make his life as comfortable and full as possible in the final months of his illness. As the end drew near in his tormented thoughts he often spoke of the prisoners that suffered and died in Provost Prison, never forgetting their tormented deaths.

On February 28, 1781, as he lay on his death bed with Annis and the children gathered around, with his dying breath he told them that signing the Declaration of Independence was the most glorious thing he had ever done, and prayed independence would soon be won. With his voice now but a whisper, he pledged his eternal love for Annis and the children. He closed his eyes and death mercifully took him. He was 51 years old.

Richard Stockton would not live to see his youngest children grown or his country win the Independence for which he had suffered so greatly while a prisoner in New York.

Thus Richard Stockton paid the cost of his avowed patriotism, fulfilling his pledge by giving his "life, fortune and Sacred Honor" to his native country. Annis watched from her beloved garden at Morven when Richard's carriage-hearse passed. She had married Richard in this same garden 26 years before, and they had spent many treasured hours planting and tending to their lovely garden.

Annis was overcome with grief for her beloved "Lucius", her pen name for Richard, and wrote an Elegy to the memory of her husband.

Morven
March 9, 1781

Why does the Sun in usual splendor rise
To pain, with hated light, my aching eyes?—
Let sable clouds in shroud his shining face,
And murmuring winds re-echo my distress;

Be Nature's beauty with sad glooms o'erspread,
To mourn my Lucius number'd with the dead.
Mute is that tongue which listening senates charm'd
Cold is that breast which every virtue warm'd

Drop fast my tears, and mitigate my woe:
Unlock your springs, and never cease to flow:
For worth like his demands this heart-felt grief,
And drops like these can only yield relief.
O! greatly honour'd in the lists of fame!
He dignified the judges's statesman's name!
How ably he discharg'd each publick trust,
In counsel firm, in executing just,

Can best be utter'd by his country's voice.
Whose approbation justified their choice.
And now their grateful tears shed o'er his hearse,
A nobler tribute yield, than loftiest verse.

But ah! lamented shade! Thy private life,
(Thy weeping children, thy afflicted wife
Can testify) was mark'd with every grace
That e'er illumin'd or adorn'd the place
Of husband, father, brother, master, friend,
And swell those sorrows now which ne'er shall end.

Can we forget how patiently he bore
The various conflicts of the trying hour;
While meekness, faith, and piety refin'd,
And steadfast hope rais'd his exalted mind
Above the sufferings of this mortal state,
And help'd his soul in smiles to meet her fate?

O fatal hour! Severely felt by me—
The last of earthly joy my eyes shall see!
The friend, the lover, every tender name
Torn from my heart, the deepest anguish claim.

Drop fast my tears, and mitigate my woe:

Unlock your springs, and never cease to flow:
For worth like his demands this heart-felt grief,
And drops like these can only yield relief.

To me in vain shall cheerful spring return,
And tuneful birds salute the purple morn.
Autumn in vain present me all her stores;
Or summer court me with her fragrant bowers—

Those fragrant bowers were planted by his hand!
And now neglected and unprun'd must stand.
Ye stately elms and lofty cedars mourn!
Slow through your avenues you saw him borne,

The friend who rear'd you, never to return.
Ye muses! Whom he lov'd and cherish'd too,
Bring from your groves the cypress and the yew,
Deck, with unfading wreaths, his sacred tomb,

And scatter roses of immortal bloom.
Goddess of sorrow! Tune each mournful air;
Let all things pay the tributary tear;
For worth like his demands this heart-felt grief,
And tears alone can yield a sad relief.

The grief at his death was general and sincere. He had been a great and good friend to all. They crowded together at his funeral to honor him.

Prior to interment, Richard Stockton's remains were conveyed to the college hall, where the deceased patriot lay in the presence of a large audience, consisting of friends, relatives, fellow citizens, and the students of the college. A funeral discourse was delivered by the Rev. Doctor Samuel Smith, then vice president of the College of New Jersey (later to become Princeton University) and John Witherspoon's son-in-law.

> Behold, my brethren, said the Reverend Doctor Smith, before your eyes a most sensible and affecting picture of the same truth, the transitory nature of mortal things, in the remains of a man who hath been long among the foremost of his country, for power, for wisdom, and for fortune, whose eloquence only wanted a theatre like Athens to have rivaled the Greek and the Roman fame; and who, if what honors this young country can bestow, if many and great personal talents, could save man from the grave, would not thus have been lamented here by you. Behold here 'the end of all perfection.'

> It was one of his earliest honors to have been a son of the college, and it was one of the first honors of the college to have given birth to such a son. After having adorned the place of his education by his talents, he soon rose to the

board of its trustees, and hath ever since been one of its most distinguished patrons.

Young gentlemen, (the students of the college) another of the fathers of learning and of eloquence is gone. He went before you in the same path in which you are now treading, and hath, since, long presided over, and helped to confirm, the footsteps of those who were here laboring up the hill of science and virtue. While you feel and deplore his loss as a guardian of your studies, and as a model upon which you might form yourselves for public life, let the memory of what he was excite you to emulate his fame— let the sight of what he is teach you that every thing human is marked with imperfection.

At the bar he practiced for many years with unrivalled reputation and success. Strictly upright in his profession, he scorned to defend a cause he knew to be unjust. A friend to peace and to the happiness of mankind, he has often with great pains and attention reconciled contending parties, while he might fairly, by the rules of his profession, have drawn from their litigation no inconsiderable profit to himself. Compassionate to the injured and distressed, he hath often protected the poor and helpless widow unrighteous robbed of her dower, hath heard her with patience when many wealthier clients were waiting, and hath zealously promoted her interest without the prospect of reward, unless he could prevail to have right done to her, and to provide for her an easy competence for the rest of her days.

Early in his life, his merits recommended him to his prince and to his country, under the late constitution, who called him to the first honors and trusts of the government. In council he was wise and firm, but always prudent and moderate. Of this he gave a public and conspicuous instance, almost under your own observation, when a dangerous insurrection in a neighboring county had driven the attorneys from the bar, and seemed to set the laws at defiance. Whilst all men were divided betwixt rash and timid counsels, he only, with wisdom and firmness, seized the prudent mean, appeased the rioters, punished the ring-leaders, and restored the laws to their regular course.

The office of a judge of the province was never filled with more integrity and learning that it was by him, for several years before the revolution. Since that period, he hath represented New Jersey in the congress of the United States. But a declining health and a constitution worn out with application and with service obliged him, shortly after, to retire from the line of public duty, and hath at length dismissed him from the world.

In his private life he was easy and graceful in his manners; in his conversation, affable and entertaining, and a master of a smooth and elegant style even in his ordinary discourse. As a man of letters, he possessed a superior genius, highly cultivated by long and assiduous application. His researches into the principles of morals and religion, were deep and accurate, and his knowledge of the laws of his country, extensive and profound. He was well acquainted with all the branches of polite learning; but he was particularly admired for a flowing and persuasive eloquence, by which he long governed in the courts of justice.

As a Christian, you know that, many years a member of this church; he was not ashamed of the gospel of Christ. Nor could the ridicule of licentious wits, nor the example of vice in power, tempt him to disguise the profession of it, or to decline from the practice of its virtues. He was, however, liberal in his religious principles. Sensible, as became a philosopher, of the rights of private judgment, and of the difference in opinion that must necessarily arise from the variety of human intellects, he was candid, as became a Christian, to those who differed from him, where he observed their practice marked with virtue and piety. But if we follow him to the last scene of his life, and consider him under that severe and tedious disorder which put a period to it, there the sincerity of his piety, and the force of religion to support the mind in the most terrible conflicts, was chiefly visible. For nearly two years he bore, with the utmost constancy and patience, a disorder that makes us tremble only to think of it. With most exquisite pain it preyed upon him, until it reached the passages by which life is sustained: yet, in the midst of as much as human nature could endure, he always discovered a submission to the will of heaven, and a resignation to his fate, that could only flow from the expectation of a better life.

Such was the man whose remains now lie before us to teach us the most interesting lessons that mortals have to learn—the vanity of human things—the importance of eternity—the holiness of the divine law—the value of religion, and the certainty and rapid approach of death. (Sanderson 3: 115)

On March 7, 1781 *The New Jersey Gazette* acknowledged his worth to his country: "The ability, dignity, and integrity, with which this gentleman discharged the duties of the several important offices to which he was called by the voice of this country are well known. In the private walk of life he was peculiarly engaging; his manners were easy, his conversation was at all times embellished with the genuine marks of a finished education, a refined taste, and a true knowledge of the world."

In Richard's will, he advised his children to adopt some denomination of the Christian faith-which one did not matter–and stay with it. He believed that distinguished abilities, station and authority were desirable as occasions of doing greater public good. He felt these qualities could bring envy and opposition, and that unless public life was pointed out by divine providence it should rather be avoided than emulated. He left his estate to Annis as long as she lived, and if she remarried the estate was to be divided among her children. She could sell property for her support or the support and education of the children. John Richard the eldest son was given the estate, including the Morven mansion, and three hundred acres. His other property in Princeton and elsewhere, including Nova Scotia, also went to his eldest son and the rest was divided among his younger son and his daughters. (New Jersey Wills) Although a Presbyterian, Richard was buried in the Quaker burial ground at Stony Brook near his home in Princeton. For many years his ancestors were Quakers, and it was his wish to be buried with them.

The majestic avenues of elms that Richard Stockton's carriage-hearse passed through for the last time were the very ones planted by him on the grounds of Morven. The row of Catalpas along the whole front every year put forth a profuse white blossom on the Fourth of July, and for this reason they are called, in this country, the Independence Tree. Here in the presence of the house in which he lived and died, these trees recall, with the sweet fragrance of their blossoms, on every Fourth of July, the memory of the Declaration of Independence, and this honored Son of Liberty, by whom it was signed. (Hagelman 58)

LIFE WITHOUT RICHARD

After Richards's death, Annis, a widow at 45, her grief deep and lasting, would forever miss her beloved "Lucius". She stayed active with four children still living at home. John Richard was the oldest at 17, now the man of the house and little Abigail was but a child of seven. Each anniversary of his death she commemorated with a poem, and she missed him dreadfully. She wrote to her friend Elizabeth Ferguson a *Pastoral Elegy, First day of Harvest 1781*:

> Can Laura forget that this day
> Brings fresh to my woe-pierced mind
> The hour that tore me away
> From Lucius, the constant and kind?

While the children lived at home, Annis welcomed visitors and involved her children in the social life she was accustomed to while Richard lived. She was a patriot in her own right as she had proven years before when she buried the Whig and State papers to keep them from falling into the hands of the British. She wrote to her brother Elias after Richard's death, "Though a female, I was born a patriot." (Bill 53)

Annis served on a committee with Lady Sterling, Mrs. Patterson, and others in the support of the Continental Army in New Jersey. Esther Reed, wife of Richard's good friend Col. Joseph Reed, along with Julia Rush and Benjamin Franklin's daughter Sarah Franklin Bache and other wives of Philadelphia society went door to door raising money for the Continental army. In a matter of a few weeks they raised over $300,000. Esther DeBerdt Reed, was born in England yet became an ardent patriot, and wrote "Sentiments of an American Woman" published in June 1780, when her youngest son, George Washington Reed, was but four months old. Esther wanted to give each man two dollars to do with as they pleased, but General Washington fearing the soldiers would use money for liquor, insisted the money be used for clothing. The women bought linen and began sewing. They delivered 2,200 shirts and personalized each one with the name of the woman that made it. Sadly, Esther Reed died only four months later at the age of thirty-four of dysentery. She was the mother of four children. Joseph Reed wrote to her brother Dennis DeBerdt in England that "I never knew how much I loved her till I lost her forever." Other wives, including Annis Stockton in Princeton, did what they could for the cause.

British General Cornwallis paid the women of America a tribute saying: "We may destroy all the men in America and we shall still have all we can do to defeat the women." Dr. Benjamin Rush (Annis' son-in-law) said that "The women of America have at last become principals in the glorious American controversy." (Corner 116)

A manifesto published in the *New Jersey Gazette*, July 12, 1780, titled *The Sentiments of a Lady in New Jersey*. With the names of dozens of other women. Annis Stockton's name appears in the effort to fund a "subscription for the relief and encouragement of those brave men in the Continental army, who stimulated by example, and regardless of danger, have so repeatedly suffered, fought and bled in the cause of virtue and their oppressed country." (Mulford, 25)

Annis was a close friend and favorite correspondent of General George Washington. She was known as the "Muse of Morven" and "Duchess of Morven". In August of 1781, Washington stopped by Morven to pay his respects as his army, and the French army of Comte de Rochambeau passed through on their way to Yorktown. Washington and Rochambeau dined with Annis on the 29th. On the news of Cornwallis's surrender, the gentlemen of Princeton celebrated with punch at Beekman's tavern, a salute of 13 rounds was fired, and later a dinner was followed by 13 toasts. One can only imagine that the illumination shining from the windows of Morven shone more brightly than any other. (An interesting historical note: when General George Washington accepted the surrender of Cornwallis, he did so on the property in Yorktown once owned by Washington's 3rd great-grandfather, Capt. Nicolas Martiau a French Huguenot, the author's 9th great-grandfather, and Queen Elizabeth II of England's 10th great-grandfather and her earliest American ancestor.)

Annis Stockton's gracious hospitality made Morven a social center. At the end of March a general treaty had been signed, the war was over. Everyone was in a happy mood and with James Madison, Alexander Hamilton and Thomas Jefferson the company and conversation must have been very lively. Among other dignitaries visiting Morven was Marquis de Chastellux, a major general in Rochambeau's army. Jefferson and De Chastellux were both devotees of Ossian from whence

Morven got its name, and when Jefferson discovered that they both admired the poet, it was, he wrote, "as if a spark of electricity passed between us."

The village was full of officers, and probably the most notable was John Paul Jones seeking adjustment of claims against the United States. The Marquis de La Luzerne, the French ambassador, came up from Philadelphia with two Counts, one Italian, the other Polish, giving a real cosmopolitan flair to society. (Bill 56)

Martha and George Washington continued to visit Annis at Morven many times over the years, and they remained good friends until Washington's death. One of Annis' poems, about General Washington, on the surrender of Lord Cornwallis, was published in the New Jersey Gazette. How highly General Washington esteemed these complimentary writings, and how much pleasure they afforded him, may be seen from the letter to her.

Philadelphia, July 22, 1782

Madam:

Your favor of the 17th, conveying to me your pastoral on the subject of Lord Cornwallis' capture, has given me great satisfaction. Had you known the pleasure it would have communicated, I flatter myself, your diffidence would not have delayed it to this time.

Amidst all the compliments which have been made on this occasion, be assured, madam, that the agreeable manner, and the very pleasing sentiments in which yours is conveyed, have affected by mind with the most lively sensations of joy and satisfaction.

This address, from a person of your refined taste and elegance of expression, affords a pleasure beyond my powers of utterance, and I have only to lament that the hero of your pastoral is not more deserving of your pen; but the circumstance shall be placed among the happiest events of my life.

I have the honor to be, madam

Your most obedient and respectful servant,

G. Washington.

(George Washington Papers at the Library of Congress, Series 4)

In late June of 1783, Princeton changed from a sleepy little village to the busy capitol of the United States. On June 21, 1783, Continental troops desperate for back pay mutinied in their barracks at Philadelphia. Three to four hundred armed troops marched on Independence Hall, surrounded it, and held the members of Congress prisoner for 3 hours. The President of Congress, Elias Boudinot, then wisely moved Congress up to Princeton, New Jersey. Annis opened Morven to Congress and her brother Elias, now the president of Congress, established himself at Morven. Elisha Boudinot, Annis's youngest brother, rode into town with his troop on horseback to guarantee their safety. Princeton gave them a warm welcome, and the college allowed them to use the library room in

Nassau Hall to hold meetings. At that time there were only twenty-two members of Congress accompanied by their wives and families, and they found lodging around the village in private homes and inns.

The festivities of July 4, 1783, were celebrations of the highest order, with the war now over, and the treaty signed. Independence had been won and Annis celebrated by hanging lamps from her cherry trees. Annis wished her beloved Richard could be there to celebrate, but in a way, his spirit certainly was. Without Richard Stockton and the 55 other signers of the Declaration of Independence taking that bold step, they would not be celebrating their new found Independence. More than 70 guests were entertained and Ashbel Green, a winner of an oration contest was invited to the dinner. "The Duchess" – as undergraduate George Washington Custis reported she was familiarly called—was in a high state. (Mulford 27)

The most exciting event of the summer was the public reception of George Washington by the Congress, who had come to Princeton to advise it on the subject of a permanent military establishment. On August 23, accompanied by Mrs. Washington, he took up his residence at Rocky Hill. Three days later he rode into Princeton. Main Street in front of the campus was full of visitors from as far away as Philadelphia. The black gowned students of Princeton surrounded the door to Nassau Hall and cheered as Washington entered. The gallery was crowded; the floor

GEORGE WASHINGTON
Engraving from the private collection of
Christina Linderman

was reserved for members of Congress; and on the wall hung the empty frame of the portrait of George II, which Alexander Hamilton's cannon ball had destroyed in the fighting of January 3rd at the battle of Princeton, six years before. Two members conducted Washington to a chair beside President Elias Boudinot, who remained seated on the platform, with his hat on his head to symbolize the superiority of the civil authority over the military. When the General had seated himself, Boudinot proceeded to read an address of welcome. From the pocket of his close-fitting coat Washington drew his carefully written reply. He read it, and the simple ceremony was over. (Bill 54)

It was a grand day for Annis Stockton, and she wrote "Ode to Washington" and sent it to Washington who was then residing nearby at Rocky Hill.

Morven, August 26

Ode to Washington

"With all thy country's blessings on thy head,
And all the glory that encircles man,
Thy deathless fame to distant nations spread,
And realms unblest by Freedom's genial plan;

Addressed by statesmen, legislators, kings,
Revered by thousands as you pass along,
While every muse with ardor spreads her wings,
To greet our hero in immortal song;

Say, can a woman's voice an audience gain,
And stop a moment thy triumphal car?
And wilt thou listen to a peaceful strain,
Unskilled to paint the horrid wrack of war?

For what is glory? What are martial deeds,
Unpurified at Virtue's awful shrine?
Full oft remorse a glorious day succeeds-
The motive only stamps the deed divine.

But thy last legacy, renowned chief,
Hath decked thy brow with honors more sublime-
Twined in thy wreath the Christian's firm belief,
And nobly owned thy faith to future time."

Annis knowing he would soon return to Mount Vernon further wrote:

"Thus crown'd, return to Vernon's soft retreat;
There, with Amanda, taste unmixed joy.

May flowers Spontaneous rise beneath your feet,

Nor Sorrow Ever pour her hard alloy.

And, oh, if happly in your native Shade

One thought of Jersey Enters in your mind,

Forget not her on Morven's humble glade

Who feels for you a friendship most refin'd.

Annis would sign the poem with her pen name Emelia. Washington wrote her a letter that was most amusing.

Rocky Hill, Sept. 2d, 1783

You apply to me, my dear madam, for absolution, as though I was your father confessor....You have reason good, for I find myself strongly disposed to be a very indulgent ghostly adviser on this occasion, and not with-standing 'you are the most offending soul alive, (that is, if it is a crime to write elegant poetry,) yet if you will come and dine with me on Thursday... I will strive hard to assist you in expiating these poetical trespasses on this side of purgatory... I will not dare to charge you with an intentional breach of the rules of the decalogue in giving so bright a coloring to the services I have been able to render my country, though I am not conscious of deserving anything more at your hands than what the purest and most disinterested friendship has a right to claim; actuated by which, you will permit me to thank you, in the most affectionate manner, for the kind withes you have so happily expressed for me and the partner of my domestic enjoyments. Be assured we can never forget our friend at Morven, and that I am, my dear madam, with every sentiment of friendship and esteem,

Your most obedient and obliged servant,

G. Washington

Washington entertained frequently and lavishly at Rocky Hill, and a return dinner for the General and Martha was held at Morven.

Annis replied to Washington on September 22, the day before the college commencement:

Oh, charge me not with fiction in my lays,
For heavenly truth stood by and twin'd the bays,
Then bid me bind them on my heroes brow
And told me fame would every sprig allow.

The commencement at Nassau Hall was a grand occasion. Congress attended and Washington was the most important guest. He made the college a gift of fifty guineas, and the trustees responded by commissioning Charles Willson Peale to paint the General's portrait and ordering that, "when finished, it be placed in the hall of the college, in the room of the late King of Great Britain"; and there it hangs today in the same room with the portraits of Richard Stockton and Elias

Boudinot. Nineteen-year-old John Richard, a graduate of the class of 1779 and now receiving his degree of Master of Arts was the pride and joy of Annis and her family.

Annis sent a pastoral directly to Washington on January 4, 1784 although bad weather prevented it from being delivered until February 10. His letter follows:

Mount Vernon Feby 18th 1784

Dear Madam,

The intemperate weather, and very great care which the Post Riders take of themselves, prevented your letter of the 4th of last month from reaching my hands 'till the 10th of this.—I was then in the very act of setting off on a visit to my aged mother, from whence I am just returned.—These reasons, I beg leave to offer, as an apology for my silence until now.—

It would be a pity indeed, my dear madam, if the Muses should be restrained in you; it is only to be regretted that the hero of your poetical talents is not more deserving their lays:—I cannot, however, from motives of false delicacy (because I happen to be the principal character in your Pastoral) withhold my encomiums on the performance.— For I think the easy, simple, and beautiful strains with which the dialogue is supported, does great justice to your genius; and will not only secure Lucinda and Aminta from wits and critics, but draw from them, however unwillingly, their highest plaudits; if they can relish the praises that are given, as highly as they must admire the manner of bestowing them.—Mrs. Washington, equally sensible with myself, of the honor you have done her, joins me in the most affectionate compliments to yourself, the young ladies and gentlemen of your family.—With sentiments of esteem regard and respect

I have the honor to be Dear Madam
Your most obedient and most humble servant
G Washington

(The writings of George Washington, Fitzpatrick, 27: 337-38)

Her appreciation of Washington continued, and in a letter in prose that she sent to him at Mount Vernon in the summer of 1787, Washington touched on the country's affairs, manners, and fashions that indicated that he had a high opinion of her outlook and judgment. On the news of his election to the Presidency she wrote a congratulatory letter. "I bless myself—I bless posterity—but I feel for you." She reverted to "the ardor that almost censured by delicacy—which impelled me to seize your hand and kiss it, when you did me the honor to call on me on your way to Yorktown." She knows he will be very busy, but she is confident that she will sometimes see him and "my dear Mrs. Washington, whom I sincerely love." (Bill 65)

Annis was one of the distinguished persons who watched the President-elect's triumphal entry into Trenton on his way to his inauguration in New York. On the lst of May, Annis sent Washington a letter saying; "Sir, Can the muse, can the friend forbear...?" She enclosed another poem to "The President General" and in part it reads:

> The Muse of Morven's peaceful shade
> Gave way to all the gay parade
> For transport of her own.
> She felt the tears of pleasure flow
> And gratitude's delightful glow
> Was to her bosom known.
>
> For erst on Hudson's whitened plain
> Where the blue mists enshroud the slain
> And heroes' spirits came,
> Anxious to seal thy future fate,
> Each in his cloud of awful state
> Pronounced thee good as well as great,
> And filled thy cup of fame.

Washington enjoyed and appreciated these tributes from Annis, and he promptly acknowledged them.

As Annis approached her middle fifties she still had her strength of mind and body, her good looks, her dominant position in the society of

234.

Mrs A Stockton
        Princeton
_____

My dear Madam,   Mount Vernon, March 31. 1789

        Upon taking up my pen To express my
sensibility, for the flattering sentiments you are still
pleased to entertain of me, I found my avocations would
only permit me to blend the demonstration of that
grateful feeling with an acknowledgement of the
receipt of your polite letter and elegant poem.

        Be pleased then to accept my thanks
for them.

        The joint good wishes of Mrs Washington
and myself for yourself and family conclude me,
                My dear Madam,
                with great esteem and regard,
                    your most obedient and
                    most humble servant

                        G. Washington

the neighborhood, and her wonderful sense of humor. George Washington Parke Custis, the grandson of Martha Washington wrote of her: "She was familiarly called 'the Duchess' from her elegance and dignity of manner." She even saw fun in the situation when Dr. John Witherspoon now a widower at sixty-seven, began to pay her attentions that were the joke of her family; and she shared their amusement when the vigorous old gentleman, married the twenty-four-year-old widow of Doctor Dill, of Philadelphia.

Washington wrote another letter to Annis;

Mount Vernon, August 31, 1788
The letter reads in part:

> Nor would I rob the fairer sex of their share in the glory of a revolution so honorable to human nature, for, indeed, I think you Ladies are in the number of the best Patriots America can boast. (A salute from the Father of our Country to one of its founding mothers and the early female patriots of America.)
>
> And now that I am speaking of your Sex, I will ask whether they are not capable of doing something towards introducing federal fashions and national manners? A good general government, without good morals and good habits, will not make us a happy People; and we shall deceive ourselves if we think it will. A good government will,

unquestionably, tend to foster and confirm those qualities, on which public happiness must be engrafted.

Washington seemed to take pleasure in his correspondence with Annis over the years and she enjoyed his letters immensely and treasured them.

All of Richard and Annis's children married well. Richard married Mary Field in 1788 and later brought her to live in Morven. They had nine children. The most illustrious was his second son, Robert Field Stockton. Richard's youngest sister Abigail would later marry Mary's brother, Robert Field in January, 1797 and reside in White Hill near Bordentown. Lucius Horatio married Elizabeth Milnor of Trenton in April, 1797. Lucious the second son was an imminent lawyer that held the office of District Attorney of New Jersey, and was nominated by President John Adams to be Secretary of War, a position he declined. The twins, Mary married Rev. Andrew Hunter, a chaplain in the Revolutionary army, in October, 1794, and Susannah married Alexander Cuthbert, of Canada.

The Legacy

RICHARD STOCKTON "THE DUKE"
Painting by Christian Gullager c. 1800
Courtesy Morven Museum and Garden

'The Duke' Carries
on the Legacy

Young John Richard helped his mother manage the estate and under the training and guidance of his uncles, Elias and Elisha Boudinot, would become a lawyer like his father before him. He graduated from the College of New Jersey in 1779 at the age of 15. In 1784, he was admitted to the bar and began his law practice in Princeton. By the age of 24 his eloquence and knowledge of common law had made him a leader in his profession, a position he would hold until his death.

The President and Mrs. Washington spent a few days at Princeton in 1790, and Annis wrote to her daughter Mary describing the events. The distinguished guests arrived at nine in the morning, with Annis, her son Richard and Dr. and Mrs. Smith attending to them on a visit to the college. At one in the afternoon there was a tea and "collation" of fruit, cake, wine and sweetmeats at Morven, and Mrs. Washington remained with Annis until the "gentleman in waiting" came to collect her to the Tavern. The next day Annis proudly received George and Martha Washington for a formal, public audience and then in private, for dinner, with her son Richard, Annis, Mrs. Washington, Dr. Witherspoon, and Dr. Smith (Witherspoon's son-in-law and President of the College) as the only guests. (Bill 64)

Annis continued on at Morven while her children grew older and married. The garden was a continual source of pleasure to her, and she entertained Andre Michaux, Botanist to King Louis XVI of France, who came to see it, conversed over a cup of tea, and offered her the seed of a Persian plum tree. (Mulford 27)

Richard's coach with the "gentle and steady" young man driving it became a familiar sight on the roads from one New Jersey courthouse to another. He represented clients in New York and Philadelphia and cases before the Supreme Court of the United States. A young man, who had seen the darkness of war and the suffering and death of his father, he had the determination to make himself a professional beyond his years. In his profession his manner was such that the younger lawyers called him the "Duke" years before his age justified that designation. He was admired for his high character, ability, and stern integrity. Those who saw only the side he showed to the world would have been amazed if they could have read the letters he wrote to his wife and children.

> Separation from my dear Mary and my sweet babe is becoming irksome to me....God bless you, my love, he writes to his wife from Philadelphia in the earliest year of their marriage; and again: My dearest Mary.....Oh! you bad girl for not writing and when they have been married for six years, he concludes a letter: Don't forget but continue to love your affectionate husband, R.S. (Bill 71)

In the midst of politics and business he thought of Morven longingly, as the place where he could find the best blessing of life: "leisure with dignity." Busy in court at Trenton the year after his marriage, he yearned to be gardening at home, feeding the chickens and searching for eggs with his "dearest Molly." At Philadelphia, eight years later, as a senator from New Jersey and with cases before the Supreme Court, he was involved in a round of dinners, dances, plays, and tea parties; he had lately dined at Uncle Benjamin and Aunt Julia Rush's in the company of the President and Mrs. Washington and the British minister and his lady; but he yearns for his "dear little girl and boy" and "to be after the ducks and chickens." In 1804, though he was to be a candidate for governor that year, he wrote to his wife, who was in Philadelphia on a visit, that he was concerned entirely with his children's happiness and the management of Morven and its farm. (Bill 73)

By 1794, Annis no longer lived at Morven, as the house swelled with the six young girls and boys, children of her son Richard and his wife Mary Field. When Washington last paid her a visit, she was boarding with a friend, and then she later moved to the home of her youngest daughter Abigail and her husband Robert Field in "White Hill" New Jersey. In her last years Annis, fighter that she was, battled yellow fever, dysentery, and rheumatism before becoming terminally ill.

In January, 1801 her children gathered round as her life neared its end. Julia Rush, Abigail, Richard and Lucius Horatio Stockton, her brother's daughter, Susan (Boudinot) Bradford (the young protester who poured tea from the window) gathered to bid her a last farewell. On the 20th of January Julia wrote to her sister Mary Hunter that their mother was dying, anxious to depart, and that she blessed them all. "Her mind was perfectly clear and rather joyous," wrote her brother Elias. "Her latter end was happy, full of peace and joy," her beloved son-in-law Benjamin Rush wrote of her in his autobiography. She died on February 6, 1801, having outlived her beloved Richard by almost exactly twenty years. (Bill 68)

On January 20, 1801 Richard Stockton "The Duke," a former Senator, wrote a letter to Senator Jonathan Dayton after he traveled to "White Hill" New Jersey, to spend time with his dying mother. President John Adams had nominated Richard's younger brother, U.S. District Attorney Lucius Horatio Stockton, Esq. of New Jersey, to be Secretary of War. After discussing the nomination and conferring with his brother while they were together, he sent a letter to Dayton at his brother's request. In this letter, Richard enclosed his brother's letter to be sent on to President Adams requesting that he withdraw the nomination. This was done by President Adams on January 29, 1801. This is a historic letter leading to the first withdrawal of a Cabinet Appointment ever made by a U.S. President, and in the 200 years since, there have been only five. Senator Jonathan Dayton signed the United States Constitution. (This letter is in the possession of the author of this book.)

Richard was well known to John Adams and was paid a compliment by then President John Adams in 1801 when Richard wrote to him about the abilities of another lawyer, whom he had recommended for an office: "I doubt, however, of his being literally at the head of his profession at the bar while Mr. Richard Stockton is there," President Adams replied. So great were his skills as a lawyer that Queen's College, now Rutgers University and Union College, had honored his attainments by making

White Hill 20 Jan'y 1801

My Dear Sir

I wrote you a very hasty line
this morning just as I mounted my horse for
this place — on my arrival here I communi-
:cated to my Brother your letter of the 17th.
his feelings are so interested that his unfortunate
measure should terminate as leave him free
of all suspicion of his being privy to it that
he has written the enclosed letter committed to you
in meant to put it into the mail of this day — It
is committed altogether to you to be used as
you judge best, either to cause the Presidt to with=
=draw the nomination, or as a resignation in
case the Senate have passed favorably on it —
considering that he has been most unfortunately
brought into public view without any act of his own
or his friends and agt his and their full conviction
of his prospects, I confess it would be most agreeable
to me that the Senate should confirm the nomination
and the letter of resignation in immediately presented.
But of this you will be the judge — I am well
satisfied that you and our other friends of

... mean to put it into the mail of this ...
is committed altogether to you to be used as
you judge best, either to cause the P. to with-
-draw the nomination, or as a resignation in
case the Senate have passed favorably on it. —
Considering that he has been most unfortunately
brought into public view without any act of his own
or his friends and of his and their full conviction
of propriety, I confess it would be most agreeable
to me that the Senate should confirm the nomination
and the letter of resignation be immediately presented.
But of this you will be the judge — I am well
satisfied that you and our other friends in
the Senate will do what is right — and be as tender of the feelings of private men and public
good will permit — My Brother begs me to
offer to you his sincere thanks for the —

friendly interest you have taken in his situation — Suffer me here again to offer you mine for this mark of your regard to us both.

I am dear sir with the great respect

Yours sincerely

R.l. Stockton

P.S. Please to seal the letter and deliver it to the President.

The Honble
Jonathan Dayton ——

Letter from Richard 'The Duke'
Stockton to Jonathan Dayton

him a Doctor of Laws.

Richard represented New Jersey in the U.S. Senate from 1796-1799 and declined to be a candidate for re-election. He was elected to Congress, serving from 1812-1815.

During the war of 1812, Richard's son Robert Field Stockton served in the Navy and won commendation for his conduct when he fought heroically in the Battle of Baltimore. Another son, 17-year-old Horatio, had joined the navy as a midshipman. When the news of the Treaty of Ghent finally arrived in Washington, Richard wrote home thankfully of the end of their fears for their "poor boys." The year was not over, however, before his young son Horatio died of injuries received in the line of duty. His body was brought home to Morven for burial. Richard chose not to run for re-election to Congress, and remained in Princeton with his wife and family. There was plenty to keep him active in private life. (Bill 76)

In 1824, Lafayette and his son came to Princeton. The College entertained them at a sumptuous breakfast in its refectory, and later in the day a diploma of Doctor of Laws, was conferred upon him. Richard had been chosen by the reception committee to make the address of welcome. Someone thought Lafayette should be addressed as "General" and not the "Marquis". Richard addressed him as Marquis de Lafayette, because as he remarked, "once a marquis, always a marquis". (Bill 83)

Richard's commitment to the College of New Jersey, now known as Princeton, was apparent as he served as a trustee for 37 years until his death. His grandfather, John Stockton, had given the college money and land to establish it at Princeton; Richard the signer, had given land, money and his dedication as a trustee for 26 years, now Richard carried on the tradition to give money, land and devotion to the college. For over four generations Stockton descendants have graduated from this outstanding University with many serving as trustees and professors.

THE COMMODORE
Engraved by H. B. Hall from a
painting by Newton. London. 1840
from the authors' private collection

THE COMMODORE

The second born son of Richard 'Duke' Stockton was Commodore Robert Field Stockton who at the age of 16, departed the College of New Jersey (against his father's wishes) to serve in the War of 1812. As a midshipman, he had earned the name of "Fighting Bob" among the sailors. He fought alongside Commodore Rogers to defend Baltimore from the British and was promoted to lieutenant for his gallantry. He distinguished himself under the command of Commodore Steven Decatur in the war with Algiers. He was liked and trusted by his superior officers, and where a task required courage, resolution, and sound judgment based on knowledge of the regulations and the law, he was chosen to accomplish it.

He was the first United States naval officer to act against the slave trade. On one voyage he captured four slave ships that had flown the French flag. He was given a reprimand by the Secretary of the Navy, but because France had outlawed the slave trade the action was later deemed correct and the reprimand unjust.

Robert Field Stockton, commanding the twelve-gun schooner, *Alligator*, set out for the coast of Africa in suppression of the slave trade. On this trip he took action inspired by his hatred of flogging. Mustering his entire ship's company on deck, he solemnly "buried the cat" by throwing the cat-o'-nine-tails overboard, and proceeded to maintain a high level of discipline without it. (Bayard 40)

He sailed for Africa once more in command of the *Alligator*. Accompanied by Dr. Ayers, of the lately organized American Colonization Society, their task was to find a more healthy location than the existing one, for the colony of liberated American Negro slaves whom it was the purpose of the society to return and establish on the continent of their origin. Cape Mesurado country, in the British colony of Sierra Leone, seemed most suitable. But the natives were ferocious by nature, and subsisted entirely on the slave-trade, with King Peter, their chieftain. After meeting with Stockton and Dr. Ayers, King Peter agreed to sell the land, and designated a time and place where they would meet. Meanwhile, King Peter made hostile by a mulatto slave trader who told him that Stockton had captured slave ships, and was an enemy to the slave trade, slipped quietly away up the river 20 miles into the interior, and Stockton was told to follow "if he dare." Stockton and Dr. Ayers accompanied only by a single seaman and a Croo interpreter followed him. The route lay through swamps and jungles, where white men had never been before. Once they found him, he had turned sullen and dangerous, his people armed and threatening. The mulatto shook his fist in Stockton's face and denounced him as an enemy of the slave trade. The seated natives now rose up and began to clang the instruments of war together and prepared to rush

Stockton and Dr. Ayers. Drawing a couple of pistols from his belt, Robert handed one of them to Doctor Ayers. "Shoot that villain (the mulatto) if he opens his mouth again," he ordered. The other pistol he pointed at the king while he repeated his explanation and persuasions. The result was King Peter later agreed to the sale, and deeded the desired land to Stockton and Dr. Ayers, and in due course it became the territory of what is now the Republic of Liberia. (Bayard 43, Bill 89)

In 1824 he started the *Princeton Courier* newspaper, wrote editorials, and made many speeches in support of John Quincy Adams for President of the United States. He had been the center of a stormy scene at the convention at Trenton in 1826, when a drunken partisan of Jackson had demanded: "What right has this damn rascal here with the Government's commission in his pocket? Turn him out!"

Robert sprang on a table and in a voice trained to be heard above the roar of a hurricane, went on with his interrupted speech. In the ensuing riot fists began to fly and he refused a dirk that someone offered him. "It's brains, not arms, that are required now," he said. But when President Adams, passed over the Old Duke and appointed another to the office of United States judge, Robert declared for Jackson. (Bill 94)

It is interesting to note that on July 4, 1826, fifty years after the signing of the Declaration of Independence, two signers of that Declaration, John Adams, age ninety-one lay on his death bed in Quincy, Massachusetts. He had struggled to stay alive until July 4, to mark the 50th anniversary of the Declaration. In early afternoon during a thunderstorm his last words to his family were: "Thomas Jefferson still survives." He could not have known that Thomas Jefferson, on his deathbed five hundred miles away at Monticello, Virginia had died shortly after midnight the morning of July 4, after whispering to his granddaughter, "Is this the fourth?" She told him it was and he smiled and shortly thereafter died at age eighty-three. Only one signer survived, Charles Carroll of Carrollton, who died six years later in 1832 at age 95.

Robert Field Stockton, along with John Ericsson, developed the first propeller driven warship for the United States Navy. He later pioneered along with his father-in-law, John Potter, the project of the canal that linked the Raritan River with the Delaware. In 1839 the Robert F. Stockton became the first iron vessel to cross the Atlantic Ocean and was then put into service on the canal. He was instrumental along with the Stevens brothers in the construction of the Camden and Amboy railroad in New Jersey that eventually would become a part of the main line of the Pennsylvania Railroad. He was nominated to be Secretary of the Navy in 1840 by President Tyler, but declined the honor. (Bill 119)

When he was home between his many absences due to his Naval service, he always celebrated with fireworks at Morven on the 4th of July, entertained distinguished guests at grand dinners, and enjoyed taking long rides on horseback with his children and grandchildren. He was generous to a fault, at one time giving a complete set of beautiful china to a lady guest who admired it, and lending money to widows and friends that never repaid him.

In winter months, the Commodore invited all his married children to join him at his Walnut Street house in Philadelphia. They shopped with "the White House ladies" who were preparing their wardrobes for the inauguration of President-elect Zachary Taylor. Taylor's daughter became known as "our Betty" in Washington society. When visiting New York they stayed at the Astor House, did their shopping at Stewart's, visited the Dusseldorf gallery, and took long walks on Broadway. (125)

In 1836 one of his many race horses, Langford, won $10,000 in a race against President Jackson's favored race horse.

As a naval Captain, he delivered the Annexation papers, annexing Texas into the United States, to Sam Houston in Texas from President Polk. Fort Stockton located in Texas was named in his honor.

In October 1845, with the new rank of Commodore, Robert Field Stockton set sail on the Congress (a fitting name) on a voyage that would "place his name in history with Zachary Taylor and Winfield Scott in the records of the war that carried the boundaries of the United States to the Rio Grande and the Pacific Ocean." (111)

On his arrival in Monterey July 15, 1846 he found Commodore Sloat who had planted the American flag but was not interested in proceeding any further to conquer California. Commodore Sloat was eagerly awaiting official notice of his retirement and his replacement. Upon relieving Sloat of his command, Commodore Stockton and his marines collected horses from the neighboring ranches, along with some civilian volunteers and sailors. This force Commodore Stockton augmented by landing as many seamen as he could spare and arming them with muskets, carbines, pistols, swords and any other weapon they could find. Meanwhile, Colonel Frémont and one hundred and sixty tough frontiersmen marched to Monterey to join Commodore Stockton, and he promptly mustered them into service of the United States and shipped them off by sea to San Diego. There they made an easy conquest. Meanwhile Stockton hoisted the American flag over Santa Barbara. Los Angeles was only 18 miles away, and he demanded of Castro, the Comandante General, that he accept independence under that flag. Castro fled in haste to Sonoma, and on August 12, Commodore Stockton led his marines and sailors into Los Angeles, with a brass band announcing their arrival. He had only been in California four weeks. (Bill 113, Bayard 110)

Commodore Stockton then proclaimed California to be a part of the United States and became its first Military Governor. A month later the Commodore opened a school and started a newspaper with his own money, each the first of its kind that California had ever known. Municipal elections were held with excellent results, and Kit Carson was dispatched overland to carry the good news to Washington.

Meanwhile, with a report that a thousand Indians were going to attack settlements in the Sacramento Valley, Commodore Stockton set sail to San Francisco to defend them. In his absence a small uprising occurred, and he had to retake San Pedro, then San Diego and marched back to retake Los Angeles. About five hundred and fifty armed Californians tried to stop him at the San Gabriel River on January 8, 1847. The Americans charged with the cry "New Orleans"—it was the anniversary of Jackson's defeat of the British in 1815—and two days later the same American flag was again hoisted over the City of Angels.

President Polk, in his annual message of December, 1846, approved and justified the proceeding of the Commodore in the most comprehensive terms. He says:

> Our squadron in the Pacific, (Commodore Stockton) the co-operation of a gallant offer of the army (Col. Frémont) and a small force hastily collected in that distant country, have acquired nearly bloodless possession of the Californias, and the American flag has been raised at every important point in that province. I congratulate you on the success which has thus attended our military and naval operations.

> By the laws of nations, a conquered territory is subject to be governed by the conqueror during his military

possession and until there is either a treaty of peace or he shall voluntarily withdraw from it. The old civil government being necessarily superseded, it is the right and duty of the conqueror to secure his conquest and inhabitants. This right has been exercised and this duty performed by the establishment of temporary governments in some of the conquered provinces of Mexico, assimilating them, as far as practicable, to the free institutions of our own country. (154)

The Secretary of War, in his annual report of the same year (1846) thus speaks of the events in California:

"Commodore Stockton took possession of the whole country as a conquest of the United States, and appointed Colonel Frémont governor, under the law of nations, to assume the function of that office when he should return to the squadron." (155)

By December 1847 President Polk and his cabinet decided to charge Col. Frémont with insubordination regardless of his earlier praise of him.

These are the facts in the case against Col. Frémont. Kit Carson testified that he told General Kearney when he met him in New Mexico, on his way east that California had been taken four months earlier. A civil government had been established and Commodore Stockton was the military governor. Carson told General Kearney he was too late, and may as well go back to Washington with him, as he carried papers to give to the President from Commodore Stockton relaying the exact information he had told Kearney.

General Kearney would have none of it, and forced Kit Carson to go with him, and headed to California looking for glory. General Kearney was instructed by the War Department on June 3, 1846, to raise one thousand men, and proceed with them across the country to California, and, "should" he "conquer and take possession" of the country, "establish a temporary civil government therein." On June 8, 1846 similar orders were issued to the naval commander in California. Therefore, both Army and Navy were told to do the same thing. (149)

Once General Kearney learned that the objects of his instructions had already been completed by Stockton, he should by all rights have turned back to Washington. He dismissed most of his men and proceeded with only eighty men to California. General Kearney's judgement seemed to fail him as he was not following the instructions by dismissing the men, and then proceeding on to California when it had already been conquered by Stockton.

General Kearney continued on to San Diego, and was attacked by Californians where 18 of his men were killed and 15 wounded. The Commodore, when notified of the attack on Kearney, immediately sent men to his aid and rescued them. When General Kearney met Commodore Stockton, probably embarrassed by the rescue, he never asked to be made officer in charge though he outranked Commodore Stockton and Stockton offered Kearney the command, but it was declined.

Commodore Stockton, and Colonel Frémont, who had conquered California while Kearny was on the way from Washington, later refused to recognize his orders over theirs, holding that the situation had completely changed since his order was issued and Kearney had not conquered California before them. Colonel Frémont assumed the governorship when Stockton departed and then the situation deteriorated. Apparently, General Kearney wanted his share of glory in California and wanted to be governor.

Before he left for his journey overland Rev. Walter Colton, chaplain of the Congress, was given charge of the newspaper. Colton wrote:

June 4, 1847

Commodore R. F. Stockton:

> To you California is indebted for her first press and her first school-house. This may not be known generally now, but it will if I live. It is something to conquer a country; it is also something to provide for the progressive intelligence of its inhabitants; but is rarely that, as in the present instance, the honor of both appertains to the same individual. (158)

This was the character of Commodore Robert Field Stockton.

Before leaving California, Commodore Stockton determined that all the debts which he had contracted for the purchase of horses, or by appropriation of other property of the emigrants and settlers, on account of government, should be liquidated. He applied to Commodore Biddle to approve his drafts on the government for that purpose; but Biddle declined to take the responsibility. Commodore Stockton, on his own authority, drew on the proper offices at Washington drafts sufficient in amount to pay all those demands which he felt bound in honor to satisfy. The drafts were all duly honored. (159)

There were no further hostilities, and in June 1847 the Commodore was on his way home–overland this time. His party consisted of 49 men of all nations, professions and pursuits. Some were trappers and hunters; some sailors; some Spaniards; some Irishmen; and French. The Commodore had ordered that Indians, who dogged the party constantly, were not to be molested. This caused great concern to the many mountain men. However, when he was shot through both thighs by an Indian arrow, he reversed his orders, and they fought the Indians when necessary for their survival. (159)

In November, after a four month journey they arrived in St. Joseph, Missouri. Here Commodore Stockton was obliged to take leave of the greater part of his men. Their parting showed how strong and sincere an attachment he had inspired in the rough mountain men. Tears rolled down the weather-worn cheeks of the hardy mountaineers, when they last shook the hand of the Commodore. They implored him to call for them if he ever endeavored to make another overland journey, and they would come no matter the hardship to be with him again. Lawless, reckless, callous, as many of them were, the Commodore had found the tender spot in each man's heart. Whether on sea or shore, few men were ever commanded by Commodore Stockton that did not become enthusiastically devoted to him. (166)

He was celebrated in every city he visited on his journey east.

When he arrived back in Washington on December 1, 1847 he did not receive a conqueror's welcome, nor could he expect one. President Polk saw nothing but political opponents in the military men who had won for him what some enemies called in derision "Polk's war." Polk a stickler for implicit obedience was unable to understand how changing conditions in war must modify decisions. President Polk and his cabinet brought Col. Frémont up on charges of insubordination.

Commodore Stockton testified in Congress on behalf of the court-martial brought against Col. Frémont along with a letter of testimony of Kit Carson and testimony provided by many others supporting Col. Frémont. Commodore Stockton resigned his naval commission and returned to his family in Princeton, disgusted with the whole situation and Col. Frémont's treatment. President Polk had the decency to remit Frémont's penalty of dismissal from service, but Colonel Frémont resigned from the army. Mexican war hero, Winfield Scott, was recalled by Polk for inquiry of his conduct in the war; it seems few, if any, could please him.

There has been some rewriting of the conquering of California in some current history books regarding Stockton, and Frémont. My next book will be to set that record straight with the documented evidence to show the real truth of California's earliest history.

> There was no obscuring, however, the brilliance of Stockton's and Frémont's achievements, let the attitude of the administration be what it might. His homecoming at Princeton was celebrated by a public meeting that passed resolutions of admiration. The New Jersey legislature thanked him for his services to the nation. Philadelphia gave him a banquet, and New York did likewise. (Bill 116)

Back in California, grateful settlers gave his name to a city and one of the principal streets in San Francisco, Stockton's name also appears on an African river and a bay south of Puerto Rico. He served his country heroically and faithfully for 38 years in the United States Navy.

Commodore Robert Field Stockton's final service to his country was to serve as a Senator from New Jersey. As a Senator he introduced legislation that would forever banish flogging as a punishment in the

Navy. He was a close friend of Daniel Webster for 30 years, and gave a moving speech to the Senate on the death of Webster in December 1852. (125) Robert Field Stockton would come close to becoming a President of the United States.

In 1851 the editor of *The Truth*, a New York publication, expressed the wish that Senator Stockton might be elected President. Other newspaper articles of the time concurred. In 1852 he was approached by various parties to see what his course would be if elected president. To all such parties his response was, that he did not want to be president, that the office was neither consistent with his happiness or his interests, but that if, notwithstanding he declined to be a candidate, it should happen he was nominated and elected, he intended to go into the office unpledged, uncompromised, and entirely independent. It seems that he would not use the office for the advancements of their interests. His own democratic party wanted to nominate him, but he again declined the nomination. (196)

His career in the Senate was short but distinguished. He was a competent, persuasive and eloquent speaker like his father and grandfather before him. He also inherited their undemanding character and somewhat impulsive temperament. He was ardent and passionate in debate and "generous and chivalric...ever ready to make amends for any hasty expression." "The Commodore is irresistible," a fellow senator said of him. (Bill 128)

He had married the lovely Harriet Maria Potter, a southern belle and heiress from Charleston, South Carolina in 1823. Harriet Maria's father

John Potter was a descendent of King Robert Bruce and the Royal Stewarts of Scotland, and his wife Catherine Fuller was a cousin of General George Washington. Interestingly, both John Potter and Catherine Fuller are ancestral cousins of Queen Elizabeth II of England through Scottish Stewart and French Huguenot lines. Harriet Maria's father, mother and brothers relocated to Princeton but still owned plantations in Charleston, South Carolina.

On his marriage to Harriet Maria, the Commodore built her a fine home now owned by Princeton University and used as a VIP guesthouse. It is known as the "Palmer House" named for one of the last owners of the home. The house was sold to Harriet Maria's brother James Potter, when the Commodore moved to Morven just a few blocks away after the death of the Commodore's mother. The Commodore enlarged Morven

Morven

HOME OF JUDGE RICHARD STOCKTON
AND HIS WIFE ANNIS BOUDINOT STOCKTON
Courtesy Morven Museum and Garden

to make it more suitable for his large family. The town of Princeton is filled with many fine homes built by the Commodore and the Potters including the "Prospect House" now used as a faculty dining hall at Princeton University.

The Commodore and Harriet Maria had nine children, and the author of this book descends from their first born daughter, Catherine Elizabeth Stockton born in Charleston, South Carolina. She married Reverend William Armstrong Dod, D.D., a pastor of the Second Presbyterian Church in Princeton. He was a graduate of Princeton, earned a degree in Law, and then became a Doctor of Divinity. He taught Architecture at Princeton University. Reverend Dod later became the rector of Trinity Episcopal Church across the street from Morven, built with money and backing of the Commodore and his father-in-law John Potter. The Commodore built Catherine and William a beautiful home that would eventually be bought in 1896 by President Grover Cleveland and named Westland. It stands more handsome than ever today in Princeton, only a few blocks from Morven.

In 1888, a statue of Richard Stockton was dedicated by Congressional proceedings and placed in Statuary Hall in the Capitol Building in Washington, D.C. One of only six signers to be so honored by his country and the state of New Jersey.

Morven passed on to a cousin, Major Samuel Witham Stockton after the death of the Commodore in 1866. Major Samuel Witham Stockton's son, "Dick" to the many who loved and admired him, had come home to die of a wound received on a battlefield in France, thus fulfilling his great-great-grandmother Annis's prophecy to the infant Dauphin:

A mighty empire from these woods shall rise

And pay to thee the aid they owe thy King.

King, Dauphin, and the kingdom had long been dead, but their country remained to receive the payment of the debt. (Bill 154)

The Stockton political dynasty was completed by the Commodore's second son John Potter Stockton. He would be the fourth Stockton to serve as a Senator from New Jersey. Morven would remain in the Stockton family for nearly two hundred years until it was sold to Governor Walter Edge in 1945. Governor Edge made Morven a gift to the state of New Jersey in 1951, instructing it be used as a Governor's mansion, or museum.

Morven would host nine sitting presidents from George Washington to Jimmy Carter, and became the Governor's Mansion of New Jersey from 1954 until 1981. Other notables who have visited "Morven" were President John F. Kennedy, Fidel Castro, Governor Nelson Rockefeller, United Nations Secretary-General U Thant, Ethel Kennedy (widow of Robert), Malcolm Forbes, Grace Kelly and her husband, Prince Rainier, and their children, Prince Albert and Princess Caroline. Morven is now a state owned museum and stands as a tribute to the lives of Richard and Annis Stockton and their descendants who occupied this magnificent and historic home.

The patriotic tradition begun by the signer of the Declaration of Independence is continued by his fifth generation great grandson, LCDR. John Glynn Jr., United States Navy who has proudly served his country under arms for 43 years. Christina, daughter of John and Kathryn Glynn, lost her husband LCPL. Michael Eugene Linderman, Jr., USMC in the service of his country in the 1991 Gulf War.

Richard Stockton is buried in the Stoney Brook Quaker Cemetery in Princeton, New Jersey with his Quaker ancestors, and Annis is buried at "White Hill" in New Jersey. Richard Stockton (The Duke) and Commodore Robert Field Stockton are buried in Princeton Cemetery.

John Glynn at Richard Stockton's marker at Stoney Brook Quaker Cemetery

THE SIGNERS OF THE DECLARATION OF INDEPENDENCE

Most signers of the Declaration of Independence are not known to the average American. Jefferson, Adams, Hancock, and Franklin are familiar names. Yet the others, in affixing their signatures to the Declaration, showed equal patriotism and deserve the gratitude of their country. They literally pledged their lives when they signed their names on that immortal Document.

These early patriots were not impractical men. They knew what they wanted. They wanted the opportunities they had found in a new land permanently guaranteed to themselves and their descendants. They wanted a voice in their own government.

The 56 signers of the Declaration of Independence had courage and a sense of purpose. They were nearly all men of means and they all had achieved prominence in their respective colony, but only Benjamin Franklin had achieved an international reputation. Most were American-born, but eight, including John Witherspoon of Scotland, were natives of the British Isles.

Most were well educated and prosperous, and for their dedication to the cause of independence, many risked loss of fortune, imprisonment, and death for treason. We must remember that the sacrifices, hardships and dangers endured by the signers fell with equal weight on their wives and families. Luckily most were beyond the path of the British army, but many of the families were scattered when the British pillaged or confiscated their homes. John Hart of New Jersey suffered the destruction of his property, and he and his 13 children were forced to leave his sick wife and hide in the forest to evade capture. She died in their absence. It is said that descendents of John Hart may be found in every state in this country. Elizabeth Lewis, wife of Francis Lewis of New York, was captured by the British and imprisoned as mentioned earlier in the book. She never recovered and died two years later.

Signers Thomas Heyward, Jr., Edward Rutledge, and Arthur Middleton were captured and imprisoned while serving in militias and defending Charleston. Thomas Heyward and George Walton were wounded in battle but recovered and George Walton was paroled before being later imprisoned then exchanged.

Only Richard Stockton was imprisoned in close confinement, starved, put in irons and brutally treated as a common criminal for signing the Declaration of Independence.

Nearly all emerged poorer for their public service. General Thomas Nelson Jr. then acting Governor of Virginia (my cousin) was at the front of the command of the Virginia military forces at Yorktown. His home was destroyed in the battle when he ordered it to be fired on to destroy the enemy within. Earlier he had helped finance the war by pledging his own estates to raise nearly two million dollars for the army. He was never repaid, his property was forfeited, and he died in poverty a few years later.

The signers of the Declaration of Independence represented many vocations. Twenty-four were lawyers, fourteen farmers, four physicians, one minister of the gospel, and three who were prepared for that calling but chose other vocations, one manufacturer and nine merchants. The longevity of the signers is remarkable. Three lived to be over 90 years of age, ten over 80, eleven over 70, fourteen over 60, eleven over 50, six over 44, and one, Mr. Lynch, was lost at sea at 30 years of age. Thus the average of the signers was over 62 years.

Most of the signers had nothing to gain materially and practically all to lose when they signed the Declaration of Independence. By signing they have all earned a place of distinct honor in the history of the United States of America. This brave and selfless act alone insured them immortality.

Signers of the Declaration of Independence

John Hancock - President of Congress

NEW HAMPSHIRE

Josiah Bartlett

William Whipple

Matthew Thornton

MASSACHUSETTS

Samuel Adams

John Adams

Robert Treat Paine

Elbridge Gerry

CONNECTICUT

Roger Sherman

Samuel Huntington

William Williams

Oliver Wolcott

NEW YORK

William Floyd

Phillip Livingston

Francis Lewis

Lewis Morris

NEW JERSEY

Richard Stockton

John Witherspoon

Francis Hopkinson

John Hart

Abraham Clark

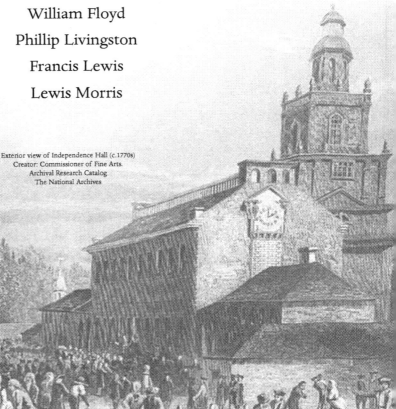

Exterior view of Independence Hall (c.1770s)
Creator: Commissioner of Fine Arts.
Archival Research Catalog
The National Archives

Oliver Wolcott Rich Stockton Benjamin Rush John Penn Wm Hooper Geo Clymer

PENNSYLVANIA
Robert Morris
Benjamin Rush
Benjamin Franklin
John Morton
George Clymer
James Smith
George Taylor
James Wilson
George Ross

DELAWARE
Caesar Rodney
George Read
Thomas McKean

MARYLAND
Samuel Chase
William Paca
Thomas Stone
Charles Carroll

VIRGINIA
George Wythe
Richard Henry Lee
Thomas Jefferson
Benjamin Harrison
Thomas Nelson, Jr.
Francis Lightfoot Lee
Carter Braxton

NORTH CAROLINA
William Hooper
Joseph Hewes
John Penn

SOUTH CAROLINA
Edward Rutledge
Thomas Heyward, Jr.
Thomas Lynch, Jr.
Arthur Middleton

GEORGIA
Button Gwinnett
Lyman Hall
George Walton

RHODE ISLAND
Stephen Hopkins
William Ellery

SACRED HONOR

Now that you have read our book, do you think that Judge Richard Stockton deserves attacks on his character and sacred honor? The attacks on his patriotism do not follow any written or factual history published at the time of the American Revolution. These accusations are based on conjecture and innuendo written by an editor in 1923.

In a current popular book about the revolution, *Washington's Crossing*, the author writes: "Stockton was the only signer of the Declaration of Independence who abandoned the American cause and swore allegiance to George III." (Fischer, *Washington's Crossing* 164) The Howe Proclamation of November 30, 1776, never required one to swear allegiance to George III, one was only required to remain in peaceable obedience. Furthermore, there is no proof that Stockton ever took the Howe Proclamation.

He further describes Judge Stockton as "turning his coat," and says that "Stockton completed his infamy" and was "a sad and pathetic figure." (Fischer, *Washington's Crossing* 164-165) These remarks have no merit, are not accurate and are an affront to the character of one who gave much for his country and personally suffered for being a signer of the Declaration of Independence. According to *Webster's New World Dictionary*, a turncoat is "one who switches to an opposing side." Stockton never switched sides or aided the British.

This author further wrote; "This signer of the Declaration of Independence now signed a declaration of allegiance to the king and gave 'his word of honor that he would not meddle in the least in American affairs'." (Fischer 164) This statement is not correct as the author interjects his opinion that Stockton signed a declaration of allegiance to the king. This critical judgement is based on conjecture, and then Fischer adds a quote from the Rev. John Witherspoon letter of March 17, 1777, in an attempt to support his charge. The proceeding information is also cited as coming from the autobiography of Benjamin Rush. That cited information is not there.

I provided the author with proof to the contrary and pointed out that his footnotes, citing the autobiography of Benjamin Rush, did not back up the information he had quoted. In his autobiography Benjamin Rush wrote: "At Princeton I met my wife's father who had been plundered of all his household furniture and stock by the British army, and carried a prisoner to New York, from whence he was permitted to return to his family upon parole." (Corner 130) The author further mistakenly identifies Richard Stockton as bringing the College of New Jersey to Princeton. Richard's father John Stockton is credited with bringing the College to Princeton in 1754, not Richard. The negative bias of this author is apparent, as he describes the departure of Rev. John Witherspoon from Princeton under the same circumstances as Richard Stockton's escape from the British Army, in that Witherspoon "chose the response of flight" (Fischer, *Washington's Crossing* 162) versus "lost his nerve and fled" (Fischer, *Washington's Crossing* 163) as Richard Stockton is described.

In another book by the same author he writes about the famous John

Trumbull painting of the Declaration of Independence and said: "Richard Stockton skulks in the background; he would be the only signer to renounce the Declaration when British troops approached his home in New Jersey." (Fischer, *Liberty and Freedom* 191) The truth is that when the British approached his home in Princeton, Richard Stockton was not there. Richard Stockton had been captured nine days earlier by loyalists over thirty miles away at the home of a friend. When Lord Cornwallis and his British troops arrived and took Stockton's house for his headquarters on December 7th, 1776, Richard Stockton certainly never renounced the Declaration to them because he sat in irons at the Provost Prison in New York and would not be released until another five weeks of brutal treatment. The Trumbull painting was done in 1818, 37 years after Richard Stockton died, and did not include all the signers, just the men Trumbull felt were most important to the event. John Trumbull felt Judge Richard Stockton was important enough to be included in the painting and certainly never painted him "skulking" in the background. This is just another sad example of this author's tendency to contrive events that never happened.

I have done extensive research on Richard Stockton's capture and release, as well as other prisoners captured and imprisoned in the New York City prisons and on British ships. The first published writings on Richard Stockton's capture and release start in 1823 with John Sanderson's *Biography of the Signers to the Declaration of Independence*. Sanderson began his book project while several of the Signers were still living. He interviewed friends and relatives of those who had died and compiled recollections of the living signers. The close reading of the many pages on each signer reveal that Sanderson did not just praise the signers but exposed controversy and flaws of the signers as well. If Richard Stockton had taken a Pardon from Howe, it surely would have been written about in this historical work and other history books of the era. Sanderson and all of the authors of that period said <u>nothing</u> of Stockton signing Howe's Proclamation, or taking protection, clearly because it never happened.

All of these negative remarks about my great grandfather are based on the Rev. John Witherspoon's personal letter of March 17, 1777. The letter was written from Philadelphia and is simply what people were gossiping about in Princeton, rumors about Judge Stockton that were relayed to Witherspoon during his four day stay in Princeton. These rumors were then passed on to his son David in the letter. A loyalist, a Mr. Cochran, had a quarrel with Judge Stockton and was responsible for spreading these rumors, according to Witherspoon.

Rev. Witherspoon wrote:

> I was at Princeton from Saturday night till Wednesday. Judge Stockton is not well in health and is much spoken against for his conduct. He signed Howe's Declaration and gave his word of Honor that he would not meddle in the least in American affairs during the war. Mrs. Cochran was sent to the ennemies {sic} Lines by a Flag of truce, and when Mr. Cochran came out to meet his wife he said to the

officers that went with the Flag that Judge Stockton had brought evidence to General Howe to prove that he was on his way to seek a protection when he was taken, this he denies to be true yet many credit it, but Mr. Cochran's known quarrel with him makes it very doubtful to candid persons. (*Letters of Delegates to Congress, Vol. 6*)

The Howe's Declaration he signed giving his word of honor not to meddle in the American affairs during the war was the parole Benjamin Rush said Richard Stockton was given when he was released from prison in New York. (Corner 130)

A Parole is a pledge of one's honor given by a prisoner of war to fulfill stated conditions in consideration of his release. An example: "Resolved, That the said committee be empowered to discharge from a Gaol (jail) ...the said prisoners first signing a Declaration, that they will not hereafter engage in such measures, nor give the enemies aid, information, counsel, or assistance (meddle), in any way or manner whatsoever; and that such as the said Committee judge proper, give security not to depart the City of Philadelphia without leave of Congress." (*American Archives, V3-p1604*). This was the language used by Rev. John Witherspoon when he and the committee agreed to free British prisoners on parole in Philadelphia.

There is a big difference between an honorable parole that Benjamin Rush stated Richard Stockton, his father-in-law, was given and a pardon or protection some authors 'believed' Stockton took. They mistake

Howe's <u>Declaration</u> he signed, a parole, for Howe's <u>Proclamation</u>, a pardon, that he did <u>not</u> sign.

Rev. Witherspoon in his letter never said he personally saw or talked to Judge Stockton and was simply passing on this rumor about a false accusation to his son as it was told to him. Witherspoon certainly never said Judge Stockton swore allegiance to the king, or signed Howe's Proclamation, or took protection, and in fact, the letter stated that Stockton had denied taking the protection.

Rev. John Witherspoon remarked, "Few persons have been less concerned than I have been, through life, to contradict false accusations, from an opinion which I formed early, and which has been confirmed by experience, that there is scarcely any thing more harmless." (Sanderson 258)

Possibly this is why he wrote the letter about the false accusation (rumors) relayed to him by some townspeople to his son. He thought it harmless as it was enclosed in a private letter. Little would he know that the false accusation in that letter would be used to destroy the reputation of his good friend 229 years later.

Richard Stockton could not have been on his way to take the protection as Mr. Cochran's rumor claimed, not only because Richard Stockton denied this but because the Howe Proclamation was not written and available until after Stockton had already been captured, turned over to the British and was suffering in prison. The absolute absurdity of this rumor is the claim that Richard Stockton would spend over six weeks in irons in the most horrible prison conditions imaginable then agree to Howe's Proclamation after his side was winning battles, turning the war around and Congress as well as General George Washington had intervened on Stockton's behalf to General Sir William Howe.

My research has found no period letters, newspaper articles, writings, etc. that say anything negative about Richard Stockton from Witherspoon or any other members of the Continental Congress. If someone of Richard Stockton's stature had taken the Howe's Proclamation of November 30, 1777, it surely would have been news worth writing about. A few modern authors, using the Witherspoon letter, have gone so far as to say Richard Stockton was the only signer of the Declaration of Independence to recant. In the dictionary 'recant' is to withdraw or disown a statement or belief formally and publicly. Richard Stockton never formally or publicly stated he regretted signing the Declaration of Independence. As a matter of fact he suffered at the hands of the British probably more than any signer of the Declaration of Independence and gained nothing for his sacrifices for his country.

These authors have also made an issue of his taking the 'oath of allegiance' as prescribed by General Washington in January 1777. The facts are: the Council of Safety of New Jersey required, among other things that, "anyone captured in New Jersey and moved into enemy lines to take the oath." (Council of Safety Minutes) Richard Stockton was captured in New Jersey and imprisoned in New York City. Therefore, he was required to appear before the Council and follow their procedures.

When someone was called before the Council of Safety, their name was given, they were questioned. It was clearly written in the minutes if they had signed the Howe Proclamation, and if so, they were at that time, required to hand in their protection papers. In the referenced abstract of the Council's minutes it states on December 22, 1777 that: "Richard Stockton, Esqr. was called before the board, took the Oaths, and was dismissed." (*Council of Safety Minutes State of New Jersey 1777-1778*) Since Richard Stockton was not listed as turning in protection papers to the Council it is proof that he did not sign the Howe proclamation as is being claimed. The Council of Safety proceeding, in addition to the letter of General Sir William Howe to the British Parliament stating "at no time had a leading rebel sought pardon," (Gruber 195) makes it very clear that Richard Stockton is not a turncoat, infamous, skulking person who recanted signing the Declaration as is being claimed in Washington's Crossing. The reckless assault on his character and reputation needs to end.

In Alfred Hoyt Bill's *A House Called Morven* he states that "Common report, moreover, may be attributed to him (Judge Stockton) some of the exploits of a distant cousin, Major Richard Witham Stockton a particularly obnoxious Tory, who did take Howe's protection and went over to the British until he was captured in February (1777)." (Bill 43) Perhaps people confused the two Richard Stocktons, and that confusion was a factor in the rumor being spread.

It is a national disgrace that a few authors and historians analyze old letters and theorize about what the writer meant to say, then write a book and include, without proof, the inferences which dishonor great men of history and attempt to rewrite our national history. Absent primary proof one should not harm the character of someone based on secondhand information.

In 1866, in a monograph entitled *Joseph Reed, a Historical Essay*, Mr. Bancroft, a historian, asserted his belief that Joseph Reed had accepted protection, under the proclamation of the brothers Howe. Reed's grandson, William B. Reed replied to this severe attack in an able argument. Mr. Bancroft attempted to sustain his opinion by quoting from the diary of Colonel von Donop of December 21, 1776, wherein the Hessian commander refers to "Colonel Reed, who lately received a Protection," etc. In the year 1876 it was discovered that beyond a doubt the Colonel Reed who did take "protection" from Colonel von Donop was Colonel <u>Charles Read</u> and not Colonel <u>Joseph Reed</u>, Washington's adjutant-general, Colonel von Donop had misspelled his name. Mr. Bancroft then acknowledged the mistake, but the damage had been done and certainly this brave patriot's reputation had been damaged. (Stryker 78)

We need to remember Herman Ausubel's wise dictum: "The historian who aspires to be a judge must not try his case by a code unknown to the defendant."

Source References

Allen, Ethan. *Life of Ethan Allen.*

American Archives. *Documents of the American Revolution.* Northern
   Illinois University Libraries.
   Website sponsored by the National Endowment for the Humanities
   and Northern Illinois University Libraries.

Bayard, Samuel. *Life of Commodore Robert F. Stockton.* New York:
   Derby & Jackson, 1856.

Bill, Alfred Hoyt. *A House Called Morven.* Princeton:
   Princeton University Press, 1954.

Bill Alfred Hoyt. *New Jersey and the Revolutonary War.* Princeton:
   D. Van Nostrand Co., Inc., 1964.
   (page 24 referencing New Jersey state officials taking Howe's offer;
   no reference to Richard Stockton)

Boyd, George Adams. *Elias Boudinot Patriot and Statesman 1740 – 1821.*
   Princeton: Princeton University Press, 1952

Brodsky, Alan. *Benjamin Rush: Patriot and Physician.* New York:
   St. Martin's Press, 2004. (page 160, exchanged for a British officer)

Commager, Henry Steele and Richard B. Morris. *The Spirit of
   Seventy-Six.* New York: Castle Books, 1958.
   (conditions of prisoners, diaries of prisoners in New York, Battle of
   Princeton.)

Corner, George W. *The Autobiography of Benjamin Rush.* Princeton: The American Philosophical Society, Princeton University Press, 1948. (page 130, parole)

Dandridge, Danske. *American Prisoners of the Revolution.* 1910 (www.gutenberg.org).

Fischer, David Hackett. *Liberty and Freedom.* New York: Oxford University Press, 2005.

Fischer, David Hackett. *Washington's Crossing.* New York: Oxford University Press, 2004.
(pages 164 and 165 – page 164 indicating that Richard Stockton signed a declaration of allegiance and references Dr. Benjamin Rush's auto biography, page 147 as the source of this information. The Rush autobiograhy on page 147 does not have the referenced information as described, and in fact, on page 130 of the autobiography, it states that he {Stockton} was paroled and has no mention of his signing any declaration of allegiance.)

Ferris, Robert G. and Richard E. Morris. *Signers of the Declaration.* United States Department of the Interior, National Park Service, 1973. (page 135 exchanged)

Ferling, John. *A Leap in the Dark.* New York: Oxford University Press, 2003.

Goodrich, Rev. Charles A. *Lives of the Signers of the Declaration of Independence.* New York: William Reed & Co., 1829. (released)

Green, Harry, Mary Wolcott Green, and David Barton. *Wives of the Signers*. Aledo, Texas: Wallbuilder Press, 1997.
(Reprint of an excerpt from The Pioneer Mothers of America published in 1912.)

Griffin II, Samuel B. *The War for American Independence from 1760 to the Surrender at Yorktown in 1781*. Chicago: University of Illinois Press, 2002.
(page 332 referencing that other than Joseph Galloway, no American of any consequence chose to take Howe's offer.)

Gruber, Ira D. *The Howe Brothers and the American Revolution*. New York: W.W. Norton and Company, Inc., 1972.
(page 196 referencing information about those who signed the Howe brothers' proclamation; no mention of Richard Stockton.)

Gerlach, Larry R. *Prologue to Independence, New Jersey in the Coming of the American Revolution*. New Brunswick, New Jersey: Rutgers University Press, 1976.

Hagelman, John Frelinghuysen. *History of Princeton and Its Institutions*. Philadelphia: 1879.

Hallahan, William H. *The Day the Revolution Ended, 19 October 1781*. Hoboken, N.J.: John Wiley & Sons, Inc., 2004.

Hawke, David Freeman. *Honorable Treason*. New York: Viking Press, 1976.

Hutchinson, Richard S. *Abstracts of the Council of Safety Minutes, State of New Jersey, 1777-1779.* Westminster, Maryland: Heritage Books, 2005.

Hess, Steven. *America's Political Dynasties.* Garden City, New York: Double Day and Company Inc. 1966.

Kelly, C. Brian. *Best Little Stories from the American Revolution.* Nashville: Cumberland House, 1999.
(page 157, parole)

Library of Congress

Linton, Calvin D. *Bicentennial Almanac.* Nashville: Thomas Nelson, Inc., 1975.

Lossing. B. J. *Signers of the Declaration of American Independence.* New York: Derby & Jackson Publishers, 1857.
(page 80, exchanged)

McCullough, David. *1776.* New York: Simon & Schuster, 2005.

McCullough, David. *John Adams.* New York: Simon & Schuster, 2001.

Michael, William H. *The Declaration of Independence.* Washington, D.C.: Government Printing Office, 1904.

Miller, John C. *Origins of the American Revolution.* Little, Brown and Co., 1943.

Mulford, Clara. *Only for the Eye of a Friend, the Poems of Annis Boudinot Stockton.* Charlottesville: University Press of Virginia, 1995.

Prudential Press Company of America. *The Signers of the Declaration of Independence.* Newark, New Jersey: 1930. (page 27, release and exchange)

Sanderson, John. *Biography of the Signers of the Declaration of Independence,* Vol III. Philadelphia: R. W. Pomeroy, 1823. (page 103, released)

Sanderson, John. *Biography of the Signers of the Declaration of Independence,* Vol. II. Nashville: R. W. Pomeroy, 1828. (page 196, released)

Stockton, J.W. A History of the Stockton Family. Philadelphia: Press of Patterson & White, 1881.

Stockton, Thomas Coates. The Stockton Family of New Jersey and Other Stocktons. Washington, D.C.: private collection, 1911.

Stryker, William S. *The Battle of Trenton and Princeton.* Boston: Houghton Mifflin and Co., 1889.

Whitney, David C. *The Colonial Spirit of '76.* Ferguson Publishing Co., 1974. (page 380, released)

ADDITIONAL SOURCES

Bancroft, Joseph Reed. "A Historical Essay."

Black, David. The Eagle and the Thistle. Edinburgh, Scotland: Font; Franklin Gothic Book.

Connecticut Society of the Sons of the American Revolution. "The Price They Paid." (page 2 of 6, released)

The Declaration of Independence. The American Book Co., 1925.

Dictionary of American Biography. Vol. City Pub. (pages 45-47, exchange/release)

Historic Morven at Princeton, New Jersey, the home of Judge Richard Stockton.

Historical Society of Princeton. Princeton, New Jersey. Copy of letter written by Richard Stockton to Abraham Clark

Limbaugh, Rush H., Jr. The Limbaugh Letters. "The Americans Who Risked Everything"

National Archives of Scotland. Edinburgh, Scotland.

New Jersey Historical Society. Archives, Documents Manuscripts, Maps, and Photographs: Manuscript Group 1221.
(page 2 of 11, traded and released)

New Jersey Wills, Somerset County, May 20, 1780, 660R.

New York Public Library. New York, N.Y.
Rare Documents (Richard Stockton's eulogy)

Office of the Lord Lyon, King of Arms, Edinburgh, Scotland.
(coat of arms information)

Scottish Record Office, Edinburgh, Scotland.

Shields-Stockton Papers. Historical Society of Princeton.

Stockton Family Papers. Historical Society of Princeton.

United States Congress. Letters of Delegates to Congress, Vol. 6,
January 1, 1977 – April 30, 1777;
Letter from John Witherspoon to David Witherspoon.
(Reference to Judge Stockton: the focus of Judge Richard Stockton's detractors, a personal, ambiguous letter relaying rumors.)

CPSIA information can be obtained
at www.ICGtesting.com
Printed in the USA
BVOW10s0207100616

451206BV00007B/50/P